HOPE AND A FUTURE

ADVANCES IN LIBRARIANSHIP

Editors

Paul T. Jaeger, University of Maryland, Series Editor
Caitlin Hesser, University of Maryland, Series Managing Editor

Editorial Board

ADVANCES IN LIBRARIANSHIP   VOLUME 48

HOPE AND A FUTURE: PERSPECTIVES ON THE IMPACT THAT LIBRARIANS AND LIBRARIES HAVE ON OUR WORLD

EDITED BY

RENEE F. HILL
University of Maryland, USA

United Kingdom – North America – Japan
India – Malaysia – China

Emerald Publishing Limited
Howard House, Wagon Lane, Bingley BD16 1WA, UK

First edition 2021

Reprints and permissions service
Contact: permissions@emeraldinsight.com

British Library Cataloguing in Publication Data
A catalogue record for this book is available from the British Library

ISBN: 978-1-83867-642-1 (Print)
ISBN: 978-1-83867-641-4 (Online)
ISBN: 978-1-83867-643-8 (Epub)

ISSN: 0065-2830 (Series)

Printed and bound by CPI Group (UK) Ltd, Croydon, CR0 4YY

ISOQAR certified
Management System,
awarded to Emerald
for adherence to
Environmental
standard
ISO 14001:2004.

ISOQAR
REGISTERED
Certificate Number 1985
ISO 14001

INVESTOR IN PEOPLE

This book is dedicated to my parents, Anthony and Faye Franklin, who believed in me before I was able to. Words do not exist that allow me to express the depth of my love and gratitude.

CONTENTS

ABOUT THE CONTRIBUTORS

Caley Cannon is the Senior Library, Arts & Culture Supervisor at Brand Library & Art Center, a unique public library focused on visual arts and music that provides services and programs for a diverse community, including a collection of over 110,000 items, subject specialist librarians, exhibitions, concerts, lectures, dance performances, and hands-on craft programs for children and adults. Brand Library & Art Center is a branch of the City of Glendale Library, Arts & Culture Department. Prior to joining the City of Glendale, she held positions as Research Librarian for the Arts at Florida State University and Savannah College of Art and Design. She received Master's degrees in Art History and Library and Information Science from Pratt Institute. She is a member of the Art Libraries Society of North America and previously chaired the Advocacy & Public Policy Committee working to monitor governmental activities affecting art libraries. Additionally, she is a member of the Los Angeles Preservation Network, dedicated to preserving the exceptional collections of Los Angeles-area libraries and archives. She is passionate about community engagement and promoting the vital role of libraries and the visual and performing arts in sustaining thriving communities.

Aryssa Damron works for the District of Columbia Public Library system. She is a graduate of Yale University and received her MSLS from the University of Kentucky. She is passionate about the role of the public library in every facet of people's lives – from early literacy to engagement with middle schoolers to college preparation to adult digital literacy classes. She enjoys bringing different aspects of literacy together to engage nonlibrary users through women's history biography projects, graphic novel book tastings, yoga and mindfulness stories, and more. She is also an avid reader and writer and reviews books, works with authors through their street teams, and writes reviews and book-related content for various websites and blogs around the country.

Angiah Davis is the Director of Library Services at Gordon State College. She completed her Bachelor of Arts in Mass Communications at the State University of West Georgia and an MLIS degree from Florida State University. Her research interests include library leadership and management, library campus collaboration with academic and nonacademic departments, and instructional design.

Jewel Davis is an Education Librarian in a PreK-12 Curriculum Materials Center at Appalachian State University's Belk Library and Information Commons. She works with pre-service teachers and practicing K-12 teachers on selecting and evaluating youth literature, using instructional technologies, and developing practitioner-based research skills. Many of her workshops and classes have focused on building inclusive classroom libraries and text sets by examining representation in youth literature. As a former high school English teacher, she is devoted to advocating for youth and promoting the use of authentic texts. She received an MA in Teaching from the University of North Carolina at Chapel Hill and an MLIS from the University of North Carolina at Greensboro.

Jerry Dear, lifetime APALA member, tackles research questions as an Information Strategist in the Magazines & Newspapers Center of the San Francisco Public Library. He also teaches in the Library Information Technology Department at City College of San Francisco. His undergraduate work in English and Asian American Studies at San Francisco State University inspired him to pursue an MFA in Writing from the University of San Francisco and an MLIS at San Jose State University. As a freelance writer, he reviews books and graphic novels for *Hyphen Magazine* and *No Flying No Tights*, devoting much of his spare time to the Asian American community and literary scene.

Paolo P. Gujilde is Assistant Head of Acquisitions at Northwestern University Libraries. Since becoming a librarian in 2010, he has worked in academic libraries in the states of Illinois and Georgia. His area of focus includes collection strategies and acquisitions. He received his Bachelor's degree in Anthropology at the University of Illinois at Chicago and his MLIS at the University of Illinois at Urbana-Champaign. He is involved in various equity, diversity, and inclusion work including serving as former President of the Asian Pacific American Librarians Association and steering committee member of the Joint Conference of Librarians of Color 2022 conference.

Jia He is a Cataloging Electronic Resources Librarian and works at the Cataloging Department of Marx Library at the University of South Alabama. She performs original and copy cataloging based on current cataloging standards and practices for all electronic resources as well as other materials. Besides cataloging, she also serves as the Liaison Librarian for International Students and provides library instruction services to international students. She earned her Bachelor of Archives Science and Master of Information Science from Tianjin Normal University, China. She then received her MLIS from University of Wisconsin Milwaukee. Her research areas include cataloging and electronic resources processing, technologies and technical services in academic libraries, and library services for international students and scholars.

Kayla Kuni is the Associate Director of Libraries at Pasco-Hernando State College's (PHSC) Spring Hill campus. Prior to working for PHSC, she worked in a public library for over six years. While working at the public library, she established many programs for developmentally disabled adults. One program, designed in partnership with the Red Apple Adult Training Center, was honored with the Association of Specialized, Government, and Cooperative Library Agencies/ Keystone Library Automation System/National Organization on Disability (ASGCLA/KLAS/NOD) Award in 2015.

Donna Mignardi is a High School Librarian at Calvert High School in Prince Frederick, Maryland. She serves on several library and digital learning committees for her district and for her state. She is also the communication chair for the Maryland Association of School Librarians (MASL) and the Secretary for MASL as well. She writes a monthly blog post for Programming Librarian with Jennifer Sturge. She is a makerspace innovator. She is known for her passion for information literacy and developing reflective and ethical consumers and creators of information. Last, but not least, she was named the Maryland School Librarian of the Year in 2020.

Meghan Moran is a Librarian at the Oak Lawn Public Library in Oak Lawn, Illinois where she primarily works on resource sharing and outreach initiatives. In this capacity, she also serves as a Director for PLOWS - The Council on Aging and on the Community Health Council for Advocate Aurora Christ Medical Center. She received her MLIS from San Jose State University. She is passionate about public libraries, community engagement, and using her creativity to enhance library services and meet patron needs.

Conrad Pegues is Assistant Professor/Public Services Librarian in the Paul Meek Library at The University of Tennessee at Martin, where he supports students, faculty, and staff with their information and research needs. He has an MLIS from Kent State University and an MA in English from The University of Memphis focused on African American literature. Currently, he is working on an MFA in Fiction at Lindenwood University. His research interests include social justice and information access as well as the conflict between race and identity politics. He has published work in the area of gender, sexuality, and black male studies. He is chair of the Equity, Diversity and Inclusion Committee of The Black Caucus of the American Library Association. He is a member of the American Library Association's Social Responsibilities Round Table and its Equity, Diversity and Inclusion Assembly.

Sophia Sotilleo is an Associate Professor and the Access Services Librarian at Lincoln University Langston Hughes Memorial Library. In this capacity, she has the privilege to teach information literacy across all subject areas and the First Year Experience course. In addition to teaching courses, she serves as an Adviser for first year students. She earned her Bachelor's degree in Business Management with a minor in Information Technology at Lincoln University. She earned her MLIS at Drexel University with a focus on Academic Librarianship. She also received a post-graduate certification at the Harvard Graduate School of Education for the Leadership Institute for Academic Librarians. Her current area of research and interest is in Embedded Librarianship, with a focus on access, advocacy, and leadership in the field of librarianship. Along with having a passion for introducing and teaching about the library to everyone she meets, she is passionate about programs that empower, educate, and encourage women to explore different ways to enhance and reach the goals they desire.

Jennifer Sturge is the Teacher Specialist for School Libraries and Digital Learning for Calvert County Public Schools. She is a Lilead Fellow, Maryland Technology Leader of the Year 2019, President of the Maryland Association of School Librarians and an Adjunct Professor of Library and Information Studies at the University of Maryland College Park. She writes a monthly blog post for Programming Librarian with Donna Mignardi. She also writes monthly for *Knowledge Quest* and has been published in *School Library Journal*. She recently became a member of the *Knowledge Quest* editorial board. She is currently pursuing her doctorate with Point Park University. She is passionate about school libraries and the positive impact school librarians can have on every child.

Vikki C. Terrile is an Assistant Professor at Queensborough Community College, the City University of New York, where she serves as the Public Services and Assessment Librarian and Co-Coordinator of Information Literacy. She earned her BA in English from Wells College, MS in Library Science from Long Island University, MA in Urban Affairs from Queens College (CUNY), and is currently a doctoral student in education at SUNY, the University at Buffalo. Her research interests include the literacy practices of children and parents experiencing homelessness, the information behaviors of Renaissance Faire performers and artisans, the role of academic libraries in addressing student food and housing insecurity, and how home is depicted in children's picture books. She is currently exploring how youth-serving librarians understand their work with children and families experiencing homelessness.

Jaime Valenzuela joined the Daniel F. Cracchiolo Law Library in February 2016. He holds an MLIS and a BA in Creative Writing from the University of Arizona. In pursuing his graduate degree, he held a Graduate Assistantship at the UA's Laboratory of Tree-Ring Research where he helped build a functioning library. He has also worked and volunteered in various library settings which include the UA's Egyptian Expedition, Freeport McMoran Inc., the Arizona State Prison Complex in Tucson, and the UA Poetry Center. He is a Knowledge River Scholar (Cohort 12) and is committed to serving the underprivileged populations of the Native American and Hispanic communities.

Adriana White is an Autistic School Librarian in the South San Antonio Independent School District. Prior to this role, she worked as a Special Education Teacher for five and a half years. She also leads professional development sessions and focused on what teachers and librarians can learn from autistic and neurodiverse adults. She earned a Master's degree in Education, with a concentration in Special Education, from the University of Texas at San

Antonio. She earned an MLIS, from the University of North Texas, along with Graduate Academic Certificates in Storytelling and Youth Services in Libraries. Her work will also appear in the upcoming second edition of the American Library Association book, *Programming for Autistic Children and Teens*. She has contributed selections on the topics of Universal Design for libraries, autistic authors, and intersectionality. She is committed to the development of autism-friendly schools and libraries, and believes that accessibility and universal design are critically important issues that we all must support and promote. She also advocates for diverse books, especially #OwnVoices titles by autistic and neurodiverse authors. Additionally, she writes a column on the topic of autistic books for the nonprofit organization Geek Club Books.

ABOUT THE EDITOR

Dr. Renee F. Hill is Principal Lecturer and Diversity and Inclusion Officer in the University of Maryland's College of Information Studies. She teaches courses and provides guidance that prepare graduate students to become information specialists who serve all information seekers.

Renee earned a Bachelor's degree in Exceptional Student Education at Florida Atlantic University. Her Master's and Ph.D. were earned in Library and Information Studies at Florida State University. Renee is passionate about and committed to researching and teaching about issues that involve examining methods for increasing understanding of diversity issues in Library and Information Studies. Her research focuses on examining information needs and information access as they relate to diverse populations (e.g., members of various racial/ethnic groups, individuals with disabilities).

Renee was awarded the LJ/ALISE Teaching Excellence Award in 2017.
She is married to Thomas Hill; they have five children ranging in age from 7 to 28.

FOREWORD

So much of what libraries do now – and have done historically – may not be well known to people who love and regularly use their local library. The family attending children's story time and spending time in the community garden every week might not even know about the computer literacy courses for older adults being offered daily or the collection of resources for small businesses that library brings out together to help economic development in the community. The faculty member who regularly visits the special collection for their research and frequently orders rare books through interlibrary loan in an academic library may not know about the wide range of information literacy courses for students or the wide range of teaching resources for faculty that the library also offers. Libraries do so much for their communities in such a wide range of areas that the most impactful and innovative activities of libraries are often unknown to everyone except those people participating in the activities.

Too often, these great innovations are invisible even within the profession, especially historical contributions. For example, while you were getting your MLIS, did you learn that:

- Libraries regularly began serving patrons with print disabilities more than a hundred years before the US government granted disabled people civil rights?
- Children's story time was originally created as a way to teach English to immigrant children and to provide time for their parents to take classes in the library to learn English or gain skills for employment?
- In many big cities, the public libraries were the first government agencies to adopt inventions, such as air conditioning, that improved health and sanitation for those using their buildings?
- Censorship of reading materials – what is in library collections and what was sold in bookstores – was common in communities around the United States until librarians directly challenged these practices and publicly codified their anticensorship stance with the 1939 Library Bill of Rights?
- During the Jim Crow era, "freedom libraries" were created in many segregated communities to ensure that nonwhite community members still had access to resources when they were not allowed access to the public library?
- When the George W. Bush administration launched the War on Terror after 9/11, the only profession that collectively stood up to the ensuing infringements on freedoms of expression and access were librarians?

The past, present, and future of modern library history is a continuous – if sometimes messy and bumpy – journey of creativity and determination in trying to make the communities we serve more equitable and more inclusive.

Not all of our institutions have always been on the right side of history for every issue, but we have collectively done better than any other institution at pushing society toward being more fair and more just for more people. Building a library and opening its doors each morning is a statement of hope that doing so will serve to further enrich the lives of the members of the community.

Yet, the stories of what our institutions have done and do now are not well known. As a result, a great many people take libraries for granted without really knowing what they are doing. Worse, many people who don't know what libraries do assume that they are no longer needed simply because they don't personally use them.

As she details in the introductory chapter, the editor of this book, Dr. Renee F. Hill, was inspired to bring this collection together by a 2018 statement from a writer for *Forbes* that Amazon had made libraries completely irrelevant. Baked into the statement was a dizzying mix of privilege and cluelessness (Amazon charges for things; libraries do not) and clearly lacking sense of the ways in which libraries contribute to their communities. But it is a sentiment you do encounter with surprising regularity, including from people who write for *Forbes*, a publication that really hates it when the government spends money to help people who aren't already wealthy.

One of the best ways we can counter assertions that libraries are no longer needed is by telling the stories of what they do, especially the ways that they help communities being otherwise underserved or ignored. And Renee has done a magnificent job bringing together 15 chapters of these exact stories – librarians and libraries changing their communities for the better, creating and implementing innovative services, collections, resources, and programs, and reaching populations who really need help. No one who reads this book will ever again wonder why we still need libraries.

It is most appropriate that a book on this topic would be Renee's first book. We first met as MLIS students and have known each other basically our entire adult lives. I have also had the honor of being Renee's colleague at two different institutions, seeing first hand over the course of the better part of two decades her enormous talents as an educator of future librarians. She is uniquely skilled at conveying the power and the beauty of libraries, inspiring students to envision how they use their careers to deliver hope to the communities that they will work with. The chapters in this book provide perspectives from a range of types of libraries in many different places, each thoughtful and often personal account offering its own unique example of the ways that libraries have been, are, and will continue to be institutions of equity, inclusion, and, perhaps most importantly, hope.

Paul T. Jaeger

Paul T. Jaeger, PhD, JD, MLIS, MEd, is Professor in the College of Information Studies and Co-Director of the Information Policy & Access Center at the University of Maryland. He is Co-Editor of *Library Quarterly* and Editor of the Advances in Librarianship book series. He is the author of more than 200 journal articles and book chapters, as well 18 books. He is the founder of the Conference on Inclusion and Diversity in Library & Information Science and co-founder of the Disability Summit. In 2014, he received the LJ/ALISE Excellence in Teaching award. Too often, these great innovations are invisible even within the profession, especially historical contributions. For example, while you were getting your MLIS, did you learn that:

ACKNOWLEDGMENTS

I am grateful to my amazing husband and children who love and support me in everything I do.

Thank you to Dr. Paul T. Jaeger, who never gets tired of reminding me what I'm capable of and has been the truest of friends and most encouraging of mentors.

To all of the chapter authors who trusted me with their work: Thank you! This has been a beautiful and fulfilling journey.

INTRODUCTION: THERE IS HOPE FOR OUR FUTURE!

Renee F. Hill

HOW THIS BOOK CAME TO BE

In July 2018, *Forbes* magazine published a short (and quickly retracted) opinion piece written by an ill-informed economist who suggested that libraries should be replaced by Amazon in an effort to help taxpayers save money. People across the globe chimed in to share an important message: We NEED Libraries!

Inspired by the fact that the masses continue to believe in the value of and necessity for libraries, librarians, and the services they offer, I set out to bring together a variety of voices and perspectives to shed light on the essential and varied roles librarians and libraries play in our world.

THE CHAPTERS IN THIS BOOK

This book contains 15 chapters written by researchers and practitioners who have committed their careers to librarianship because they believe in its transformative power. Each offering contains a message that convincingly expresses how libraries serve as information centers, community hubs, and, sometimes, lifesavers.

The book's first section "Hope is Part of the Plan" begins with a chapter written by *Vikki C. Terrile*, which aptly addresses the theme of this edited volume with its strong reference to Emily Dickinson's poem *Hope is the Thing with Feathers*. Throughout the chapter, Terrile recounts experiences that illustrate the many ways that libraries and librarians positively impact information seekers. Next, *Donna Mignardi and Jennifer Sturge* collaborate to explain the power K-12 school librarians have to expand the concept of information literacy by teaching students how to recognize their own implicit biases. Following Mignardi's and Sturge's youth-focused chapter, *Aryssa Damron's* writing outlines how the public library can be a source of hope for students who need assistance with achieving their college admission goals.

The second section, "Diverse and Inclusive," presents perspectives on the myriad ways the people, services, and programs offered through libraries help information seekers feel welcome. First, *Paolo P. Gujilde* challenges academic librarians to move beyond buzzwords and be inclusive and intentional when planning services for diverse populations. *Sophia Sotilleo* considers the ways in which academic libraries can embrace all users by treating them like honored guests. *Jia He's* research shares the processes that her university's library engages in to fully include international students. *Kayla Kuni* offers personal reflections and best practices for serving adults with developmental disabilities who visit the library. The section concludes with *Jewel Davis's* chapter highlighting strategies that can be implemented to build collections in K-12 libraries and classrooms that reflect and promote diversity in youth literature.

The book's third section, "Creating Community," contains chapters that focus on the impact libraries have on the communities in which they are positioned. The section opens with *Conrad Pegues's* work which focuses on the role of urban libraries in addressing the problem of information access deserts. The second chapter in the section was written by *Caley Cannon* who presents libraries as public spaces that have a number of dynamic capabilities, including as venues where community members can participate in visual and performing arts programs. *Adriana White* positions libraries as important spaces for adults with autism – those who are patrons as well as those who are information providers.

The fourth and final book section, titled "The Future is Waiting," places emphasis on the idea that partnerships between libraries and community members can and should be in a state of constant expansion and evolution. In the first chapter in this section, *Jerry Dear* sheds light on the bridges that can be built when public libraries engage in multi-institutional collaborations. Next, *Jaime Valenzuela* outlines his experiences with digitization projects and encourages library professionals to seek opportunities that allow them to chart their own path for career success. *Angiah Davis* then shares examples of how librarians and libraries have the power to transform people and, through that positive impact, entire communities. The book closes with *Meghan Moran's* uplifting chapter that encourages librarians to become involved in their communities in order to impart forward thinking ideas that ensure information (and other) needs are met and that libraries will be viewed as essential spaces.

At its core, this book is meant to be positive, uplifting, and joyous. It celebrates a much beloved institution and honors people who have dedicated their careers to serving others through excellence in information provision. Most importantly, this book encourages all information specialists to always remember their "why" as they consider what inspires and motivates the authors of the chapters that follow.

SECTION 1

HOPE IS PART OF THE PLAN

CHAPTER 1

THE THING WITH FEATHERS: SMALL MOMENTS, HOPE, AND PURPOSE IN A CAREER IN LIBRARIES

Vikki C. Terrile

ABSTRACT

This chapter looks back over my more than 20 years as a librarian, considering how the often unexpected opportunities I've had to work with youth and families have been centered in connectedness, hope, and love. As a youth services librarian working in the library with families or providing outreach to the most vulnerable members of the community, and currently as a community college librarian, I can think back over my career in libraries, the people I've met, the experiences I've shared, and feel blessed. But there are also times I feel like Sisyphus, pushing the rock that continues to roll back on me. It is disheartening to see the same struggles getting worse in our communities, to have to fight to keep our doors open every time there is a budget crunch, to hear our work diminished by others. But I have come to understand that having hope doesn't mean not understanding how trying times are or passively accepting the ways things are until they magically change. Hope means pushing through anyway, stubborn in our love for our patrons and our peers, in our belief that books and reading can help us through, in our faith that the world needs libraries.

Keywords: Connectedness; library users; outreach; reading; community; love

Hope and a Future: Perspectives on the Impact that Librarians and Libraries Have on our World
Advances in Librarianship, Volume 48, 3–12
Copyright © 2021 by Emerald Publishing Limited
All rights of reproduction in any form reserved
ISSN: 0065-2830/doi:10.1108/S0065-283020210000048001

"Hope" is the thing with feathers –
That perches in the soul –
And sings the tune without the words –
And never stops – at all –
–Emily Dickinson (1891)

CONNECTIONS

It is perhaps oversimplifying things to say that we live in trying times; you'd have to have been living under a rock to have missed that. If nothing else, these are also paradoxical times, with huge gaps in equality, opportunity, and even our involvement with others. For libraries, librarians and other library workers, we have the privilege and the challenge of having a front row seat for these times. Only we're not sitting, we're there, standing shoulder to shoulder with our patrons as they endure political and personal upheaval. Often while traveling throughout the United States, we will visit the local public libraries. Once, outside a small library in California, a man who had just left the library chatted with us for quite some time while we were sitting on a bench out front. When we left him to head to dinner, I commented that I was sure every staff member in that library knew this man well, that he was one of the many for whom the library becomes a key source of human connection. I am not sure when I understood that libraries could and do play this role. As a frequent user of the public library as a child, I rarely interacted with the librarians (who seemed terrifying) or other staff (who seemed judgmental about my book choices), especially when self-check-out became a reality. For me, a shy avid reader, the treasure of the library was being able to wander around on my own, essentially ignored by the staff, find an armload of books, check them out and leave. Even now, my trips to my local public library branch look similar. I retrieve my reserved materials from a wall of books, use the self-check machine to borrow them, and do not ever have to interact with a human being. Yet we know that most of us often prefer to get our information from other people, a truism supported by a wide range of literature in information behavior (see, e.g., Genuis, 2015; Lloyd & Olsson, 2019; McKenzie, 2003; Zimmer & Henry, 2017). A study I conducted recently with community college students indicated that while they were constant users of "Mr. Google" (as one student described it), they were nearly as likely to ask friends, classmates, or authority figures for information.

It is worth noting that a recent, award-winning student research project that explored creating casual chatting space (based on the booth used by Lucy in the Peanuts cartoons) was situated in the university main library (Panesar, 2019). The goal of the project was to "explore whether 'casual chat' is a viable means of community mental health self-support" (Talking Booth, 2019), which also considered "how community members can support each other without professional intervention" (CPASS, 2019). In an email with the student, M. Zielinka, she explained that the selection of the library as the space for this booth was a practical one: it was a large enough indoor space where she "felt that students coming to the library would have more liberty in choosing to engage with us for a bit" (personal communication, November 21, 2019). However, Zielinka did observe that "students/staff coming and going from the library are not expecting to be invited to sit and have a chat" (personal communication, November 21, 2019). With only 16–20% of American teens and adults "unplugging" every day, and 33–43% never doing so (McCarthy, 2014, 2016), there may be a sense that we are always and well connected. Americans spend nearly two hours a day on social media (GlobalWebIndex, 2019), compared with roughly 15 minutes a day reading (offline) for pleasure, and 38 minutes a day socializing (in "real life") with others (Bureau of Labor Statistics, 2019). Research finds that passive use of social media can impact individuals' well-being negatively by promoting envy and social comparison (Verduyn, Ybarra, Résibois, Jonides, & Kross, 2017), often depending on the individual's existing state of mind (de Vries, Möller, Wieringa, Eigenraam, & Hamelink, 2018). This may be especially problematic for young people, who tend to experience both social media and loneliness more than older generations (Pittman & Reich, 2016), making them potentially more likely to have negative affective experience via social media.

If my experience as a library user has not been one that turns on connectedness, my experience as a librarian has been quite the opposite. It seems that the most important turning points in my career were accidental, or at least unplanned. Looking back to those days 25 years ago when I was applying to library school, I could never have imagined the experiences I have had, the relationships of which I have been a part. I applied to library school with the intent of becoming an archivist; as an undergrad, I had visited my small liberal arts college's even smaller and wonderfully eclectic archives, and learned (to my utter amazement) that there were people who got to work with such collections as a career. Interestingly, I became disenchanted with archival work when I realized that I would be spending much of my day alone. Having worked my way through library school as a retail sales associate, I had become accustomed to near-constant human interaction. I had regular customers and spent a good deal of time listening to the problems of my colleagues, a mix of middle-aged and young adult women. And for all of my introversion, I realized I wanted to be around people in a meaningful way, even if I wasn't sure at the time what that would mean. As a student in library school, I wrote a paper (I don't recall for which class) about progressive librarianship. I was enamored of the copies of *Progressive Librarian*, the journal of the Progressive Librarians Guild, housed in the library school's small library. I also cannot recall the focus of this paper, but I distinctly remember being told by the professor that progressive librarianship was essentially dead, a fossil from a more radical time. I wonder now what made him believe that, and how in-touch he could have been with the world of librarianship outside our school, but even then, I knew that wasn't accurate, and the sense of what libraries could mean lingered in the back of my head.

My first job in libraries was as a children's librarian in a small, suburban library. The community was economically stratified by major roads and highways that ran east–west through the school district the library served. The library itself was located in the southernmost layer of the community, a few blocks from the beach. The patrons we saw most often lived within easy walking distance, although, this being the suburbs, they were more likely to drive to the library. When we would do school visits to the district's two elementary schools to promote summer reading, it was clear that this stratification was impacting library use. In the school closest to the library, my colleagues and I recognized most of the students and were recognized in turn (excitedly by the youngest students, and with visceral embarrassment by the oldest ones). At the school located across all three of the roads intersecting the district, we would barely recognize any students. This distance of no more than two miles was enough to limit students' access. I was reminded that one summer when I was very young (no more than six or seven), my own local public library had offered school buses to bring kids back and forth to the library. My sister and I had walked to the distant bus stop with our older neighbors, library cards in hand, and we traveled what seemed so far (but turns out to be just two and a half miles) to select and return our books. I shared this story with my colleagues years later, and we brainstormed ideas for getting a bus to reach those kids we never saw. Like my skeptical professor, my head of department didn't understand why there was a need for us to bridge that distance, believing it was up to the parents to bring their children to us (or not).

WHAT WE SAY AND DO MATTERS

Early in my career, I was part of a multisession "new librarians" training at the county cooperative library system. I remember almost nothing about these sessions except for one thing, spoken by the director of the system at the time: "librarians are subversives." I was struck by this on so many levels and it stayed with me and deeply influenced my understanding of librarianship, despite the odd looks I got from colleagues when I would gush about the director and this sentiment. Years later, this same man happened to be teaching a class at another library system where I was working. One morning, I saw him sitting in the lobby waiting for someone to unlock the room he was using and I knew I had to take my chance. I went up to him and said:

> You're going to think I'm crazy, but ten years ago, I was a new librarian, and you spoke and you talked about librarians being subversive and I have to tell you that those words have been a guiding force in my career ever since. So I had to thank you!

And he looked at me, stunned, and asked me to tell me who I was and where I worked and how I had gotten here. We chatted for a few minutes and it was one of those profound moments that arrive unexpectedly in life. Later, I learned that he retold the story to the librarians in his class, and I have used that example myself when training pre-service and in-service librarians. I know he didn't remember that day – he likely did that welcome speech twice a year, every year during his tenure as director and that line may have been a throwaway. But that line became the guiding force for at least one person out of all of those new librarians. Once, I was walking down the main shopping avenue near the central library where I was working, and a man started yelling and waving. I ignored him and he ran to catch up with me. He started thanking me and talking about what I had done for him and his sister and while I started to say I didn't remember him, I stopped myself, racking my brain. At that point, I had been doing outreach for many years, across several boroughs of New York City and I could have met him anywhere. In the end, I figured out that they had been residents at a family shelter I visited to provide library cards and information, but I was struck by how important that interaction was for him. When I talk to new (and not so new librarians) about the vital emotional roles we often (and often unknowingly) serve for people, I share these two stories together, and I talk about how we don't know how our words and actions will impact people. A smile, a small kindness, a gentle word can be of immense importance to someone and we might never know. But sometimes, we are lucky enough to get a moment of grace when we discover how we have influenced someone.

READING AND BEING HEARD

One of my most successful programs as a children's librarian was a parent–child book discussion group I started for tweens and their parents. I usually had half a dozen families, a good mix of daughters and sons and moms and dads; we would meet one evening a month for four months, talking about a different book each time. I offered the program in the fall and spring for two years, and after the fourth series, the families decided they wanted to keep it going past the four weeks, so they arranged to reserve the meeting room and took turns bringing snacks and invited me for each session as the special guest librarian. As an undergraduate English major, an avid reader with friends who also loved books, and now as a librarian, I loved being able to talk about books nearly all the time. But the book discussion group was the first time I truly understood the ways that reading could connect people and give them hope. One of the moms shared her belief that the reason her son had stopped needing extra support in reading was because they had been part of the book discussion group. I'm not sure this would stand up to empirical evaluation, but even though not everyone always finished the books, and we would often get started talking about topics not even tangentially related to the book, we had created a community around reading. In that community, the voices of the children were as important (if not more important) than those of the adults, and given everything I have experienced as a librarian since then, I know how important that was.

I mentioned that most of the turning points in my career were accidental; that was certainly the case with becoming an outreach librarian. It was something I had thought about as far back as library school with that paper on progressive librarianship, and yearned to do as a way to bridge that enormous two-mile gap that was limiting kids' access to my suburban library. But it wasn't until I had moved back to New York City that I had the unexpected opportunity to really do outreach. And I was conned into it. On my first day as a teen librarian in the main branch library, my new supervisor forwarded a voice message to me and explained that it was from some man who wanted to do something with teens and seniors or something. She was a bit vague but it sounded interesting so I called the man back and he explained that he was the principal at a state detention center for young women and was interested in having the library come in to provide books and programs for the girls. Needless to say, I was stunned, but agreed to travel the couple of subway stops to the center with one of my colleagues and see what we could do. Nearly 15 years later, I can still recall, vividly and viscerally, how I felt leaving the detention center after that first meeting. I was drained, saddened to the core of myself, but immediately and fully committed to providing library services to the best of my ability to the young women in residence. I can also say with complete certainty, that that call and that meeting changed my life. I would not be the librarian or person I am if I hadn't started visiting that detention center and the many others that followed. I wouldn't have begun offering library services to homeless shelters, to young people with emotional disturbances, to men in a minimum-security prison. I would never have understood the deep and lingering social inequity of our society and looked for how libraries could be part of the work to offer access and equity. At a time when Google and Amazon were poised to revolutionize information, as bookstores were closing their doors and libraries struggling to convince politicians of our relevance, I saw first-hand how books could connect people, even (especially?) those who were excluded from so much of the rest of mainstream society.

Our visits to the detention center always included bringing books for the young women. We were limited to what they were permitted by the facility to read, and what we were able to find or request in the week between our visits. But we always brought something. During that first visit, the principal described how the girls were handcuffed and shackled anytime they left the facility. This particular detention center was a double brownstone on a residential street, so it had limited internal security and reminded me in some ways of the house the girls lived in on "The Facts of Life" or my college dorms. School took place in the same building and it was through the school that we did our programming. But the illusion of a typical dorm was shattered one day on my way in with an armload of books for that week's visit. One of the young women who had joined the library program (the girls were allowed to choose to participate and would be pulled out of their classes for our visit) was waiting in the entryway to attend a court hearing. She was handcuffed and shackled, wearing a uniform that looked eerily like a private school shirt and skirt and while I was shocked at the sight of her, she was thrilled that I had brought the books she had requested the previous week, and that I had remembered her name after meeting her just one time. So while she chattered excitedly about what she would read when she got back, I responded and then felt like someone had punched me in the stomach. I felt myself tearing up, heartbroken and appalled at the way this child was in chains, and I struggled to keep it together. It was common for the girls to show surprise and grudging respect that we remembered their first names and once we understood the ways the systems in which they were entrenched sought to dehumanize them, we were even more deliberate in making sure we knew and used their names.

Years later, I facilitated several short story discussions for teens through the public school that serves students in detention. These visits were arranged through the school's library coordinator and fit in with the English language arts units on short fiction. I used the stories from and facilitation techniques developed by People & Stories/Gente y Cuentos (https://peopleandstories.org/). In these sessions, I would read the story aloud while the participants read along (or not, their choice) and then facilitated discussion using the participants' lived experiences as the springboard for understanding the story. During one visit, the librarian advised me that the next class was very small and included a young woman who had clearly been deeply traumatized. She would move her desk to a corner of the room so that no one could come up behind her and would rarely engage or make eye contact and would often explode if pushed. A little apprehensive, I waited for the class to arrive. When it did, it was just this one young woman, her two English teachers, and the two staff members from her detention center who stayed with the students throughout the school day. As predicted, the student moved her desk away from the rest of us, into the corner, while I tried not to panic over how I was going to do this session. Incredibly, the student eagerly and actively engaged in the discussion of the story, providing insights from her own experiences and bravely setting boundaries about things she would not discuss. She was so impressive, one of the staff explained to her that this was what college was like and that she would be amazing in that kind of academic setting one day. After the session, I went to use the ladies room and one of the English teachers was there and she started to cry, explaining what a gift that had been, which made me cry, too. There were tears and hugs and the understanding from two women who had both devoted their lives to young people and reading books, that we had witnessed something rare and beautiful made possible by good literature and a safe space.

LOVE AND SERVICE

During a meeting with public librarians interested in community and social services in libraries, the social worker facilitating the event talked about approaching our patrons with love. This was the first (and still the only) time I had heard this recommendation in my career in libraries and I was humbled and moved by it. I was eager to bring it to my own training and work with in-service librarians and during my next meeting, brought it up as an approach to service. It was not well received. Several librarians commented that they didn't even *like* their patrons, how could they love them? This struck me as almost as powerful as the original directive to approach patrons from love. Does one have to be likeable to deserve love? And it certainly made me concerned about the level of service we were offering if our librarians had no compulsions about admitting their disdain for our patrons. Even now, in my community college library, a number of my peers have commented in meetings that they are afraid of our students. This is troubling and makes me wonder how we can provide truly effective service and support to students in an environment where they are perceived as frightening. I would argue that our dislike or fear of patrons say more about us and our own biases than about library users. I would also argue that meeting those biases and those users with love may be the only way to serve.

In many ways, the resistance to thinking about love as a guiding force in librarianship is connected to our professional alliance with reason and cognition. The "affective turn" within library and information science is still fairly recent (Fourie & Julien, 2014) and even then, it is not explicitly about big emotions like love and hope. For related service professionals, including nurses, social workers, and teachers, understandings of love and compassion are a bit more common, but still fraught. Smith (2011), writing about the role of love in social work with children and youth, explains that "love in its different guises … is a central component of any helping response undertaken in the context of caring relationships" (p. 189). Paulo Freire's focus on love is oft cited in discussions of critical and liberatory pedagogy, as noted by both Darder (2011) and Mark Smith (2011). Darder (2011) also notes that:

> Freire placed great significance on our ability to live joyfully despite the multitude of external forces that constantly challenge our humanity. The indispensable quality of teaching with a joy of living personifies most the ultimate purpose in both Freire's work and life. (p. 192)

This is especially telling when one considers how infrequently words like love and joy are used to describe librarianship or library work. Perhaps not surprisingly, when love is mentioned within librarianship, it is in the context of Christian librarianship; M. Smith (2011) notes a similar pattern in social work commentary. G. A. Smith (2002) notes that "identifying love as the core virtue of librarianship represents a radical departure from secular approaches to library ethics" (p. 50). Further, he argues that (Christian) librarians should be "providing loving service" (G. A. Smith, 2002, p. 48).

While librarianship may not be ready to embrace fully the ideals of loving service, there are promising practices within our field and other service professions we can draw from. For example, person-centered care is increasingly a goal in health care, even if it is not clearly defined or understood. Sharp, McAllister, and Broadbent (2016) explain that person-centered care "is responsive and adaptable to the unique needs of the individual, and based on the formation of therapeutic relationships" (p. 301). This is quite similar to how Mon and Harris (2011) describe the needs of contemporary library users who are looking for personal connections with librarians. They note that "throughout the research literature, themes abound of the importance of librarians affirming their personal presence, warmth, and humanity" (Mon & Harris, 2011, p. 359). Sharp et al. (2016) found that "a foundation of good care for [their study] participants was the feeling that nurses really knew them as people and recognised [sic] their individuality" (p. 305). Similarly, Mon and Harris (2011) describe the impact that simply exchanging names can have during a library transaction. Mon and Harris (2011) explore a number of reasons why librarians are frequently anonymous and unnamed, most of which echo Mark Smith's (2011) observations that notions of professionalism are often used to hide behind and avoid personal connection. Similarly, he points out that "more often than not, what we call boundaries are actually barriers" (p. 191) which prevent authentic connection to those we work with and serve. For nurses, the establishment of the therapeutic relationship, which does not need a long time for development, is key to person-centered care. Sharp et al. (2016) explain that "Nurses who invested in therapeutic relationships brought something of themselves to the encounter that made them more 'human' than clinical" (p. 308). This relates directly to the connectedness described by Mon and Harris (2011) as well as the growth of "personal" librarians, especially on college campuses. For example, one personal librarian project described their goal as "to cultivate deep personal engagement between the distance education librarian and the students" (England, Lo, & Breaux, 2018, p. 4). Thus, we are increasingly recognizing the need to make librarianship personal.

CONCLUSIONS

When I think back over my career in libraries, the people I've met, the experiences I've shared, I feel blessed. But there are also times I feel like Sisyphus, pushing the rock that continues to roll back on me. It is disheartening to see the same struggles getting worse in our communities, to have to fight to keep our doors open every time there is a budget crunch, and to hear our work diminished by other educators (Peet, 2019). Yet, when it all seems like too much, and too much for libraries and librarians to take on, I am reminded that, as Darder (2011) notes:

> For Freire, there was no questioning that he, others, and the world were always in a state of becoming, of transforming, and reinventing ourselves as part of our human historical process. This belief served as the foundation for his unrelenting search for freedom and his unwavering hope in the future. (p. 188)

Having hope doesn't mean not understanding how trying times are or passively accepting the ways things are until they magically change, it means pushing through anyway. I came across this quote recently: "I'm pretty sure that's what hope is. Stubbornness. Refusing to go down" (Bancroft, 2018, p. 93) which sums up what I think about hope, too. We have to be stubborn in our love for our patrons and our peers, in our belief that books and reading can help us through, in our faith that the world needs libraries.

REFERENCES

Bancroft, J. (2018). *Arm of the sphinx* (First trade paperback edition). New York, NY: Orbit.

Bureau of Labor Statistics. (2019). Average hours per day spent in selected leisure and sports activities by age. Retrieved from https://www.bls.gov/charts/american-time-use/activity-leisure.htm. Accessed on December 5, 2019.

CPASS. (2019). *CPASS student awarded PCCS books student prize*. The University of Edinburgh. Retrieved from https://www.ed.ac.uk/health/news/student-research-prize-in-cpass. Accessed on November 18, 2019.

Darder, A. (2011). Chapter 9: Teaching as an act of love: Reflections on Paulo Freire and his contributions to our lives and our work. *Counterpoints, 418*, 179–194. Retrieved from www.jstor.org/stable/42981647

de Vries, D. A., Möller, A. M., Wieringa, M. S., Eigenraam, A. W., & Hamelink, K. (2018). Social comparison as the thief of joy: Emotional consequences of viewing strangers' Instagram posts. *Media Psychology, 21*(2), 222–245.

Dickinson, E. (1891). *"Hope" is the thing with feathers—(314) by Emily Dickinson* [Text/html]. Poetry Foundation. Retrieved from https://www.poetryfoundation.org/poems/42889/hope-is-the-thing-with-feathers-314. Accessed on December 6, 2019.

England, E., Lo, L., & Breaux, A. (2018). The librarian BFF: A case study of a cohort-based personal librarian program. *Journal of Library & Information Services in Distance Learning, 12*(1–2), 3–12.

Fourie, I., & Julien, H. (2014). Ending the dance: A research agenda for affect and emotion in studies of information behaviour. In T. D. Wilson (Ed.), *Proceedings of ISIC, the information behaviour conference*, Leeds, 2–5 September, 2014: Part 1 (paper isic09). Retrieved from http://InformationR. net/ir/19-4/isic/isic09.html (Archived by WebCite® at http://www.webcitation.org/...)

Genuis, S. K. (2015). The transfer of information through word of mouth is powerful: Interpersonal information interactions. In T. D. Wilson (Ed.), *Proceedings of ISIC, the information behaviour conference*, Leeds, 2–5 September, 2014: Part 2 (paper isic29). Retrieved from http:// InformationR.net/ir/20-1/isic2/isic29.html (Archived by WebCite® at http://www.webcitation. org/6WxIuAVqN)

GlobalWebIndex. (2019, June 26). Average time per day spent by online users on social media in 2018, by country (in hours.minutes) [Graph]. *Statista*. Retrieved from https://www.statista.com/statistics/270229/usage-duration-of-social-networks-by-country/. Accessed on December 5, 2019.

Lloyd, A., & Olsson, M. (2019). Untangling the knot: The information practices of enthusiast car restorers. *Journal of the Association for Information Science & Technology, 70*(12), 1311–1323. https://doi.org/10.1002/asi.24284

McCarthy, N. (2014, August 20). People rarely unplug from technology [Digital image]. Retrieved from https://www.statista.com/chart/2598/people-rarely-unplug-from-technology/. Accessed on December 5, 2019.

McCarthy, N. (2016, March 2). How often do Americans try to unplug? [Digital image]. Retrieved from https://www.statista.com/chart/4442/how-often-do-americans-try-to-unplug/. Accessed on December 5, 2019.

McKenzie, P. J. (2003). A model of information practices in accounts of everyday-life information seeking. *Journal of Documentation, 59*(1), 19–40.

Mon, L., & Harris, L. (2011). The death of the anonymous librarian. *The Reference Librarian, 52*(4), 352–364.

Panesar, S. (2019). The importance of human connection. *Healthcare Counselling & Psychotherapy Journal, 19*(4), 6. Retrieved from http://search.ebscohost.com.qbcc.ezproxy.cuny.edu/login.aspx? direct=true&db=a9h&AN=139281005&site=ehost-live&scope=site

Peet, L. (2019). Tenured library faculty laid off at St. Cloud State University. *Library Journal*. Retrieved from https://www.libraryjournal.com?detailStory=Tenured-Library-Faculty-Laid-Off-at-St-Cloud-State-U. Accessed on December 6, 2019.

Pittman, M., & Reich, B. (2016). Social media and loneliness: Why an Instagram picture may be worth more than a thousand Twitter words. *Computers in Human Behavior, 62*, 155–167.

Sharp, S., McAllister, M., & Broadbent, M. (2016). The vital blend of clinical competence and compassion: How patients experience person-centred care. *Contemporary Nurse, 52*(2–3), 300–312.

Smith, G. A. (2002). The core virtue of Christian librarianship. *The Christian Librarian, 45*(2), 47–51.

Smith, M. (2011). Love and the child and youth care relationship. *Relational Child and Youth Care Practice, 24*(1–2), 189–192.

Talking Booth. (2019). Talking Booth wins student research prize. Retrieved from https://www. bacp.co.uk/news/news-from-bacp/2019/19-june-talking-booth-wins-student-research-prize/. Accessed on November 18, 2019.

Verduyn, P., Ybarra, O., Résibois, M., Jonides, J., & Kross, E. (2017). Do social network sites enhance or undermine subjective well-being? A critical review. *Social Issues and Policy Review, 11*(1), 274–302.

Zimmer, J. C., & Henry, R. M. (2017). The role of social capital in selecting interpersonal information sources. *Journal of the Association for Information Science & Technology, 68*(1), 5–21. https:// doi.org/10.1002/asi.23577

CHAPTER 2

CHECK YOUR BIAS AT THE SCHOOL LIBRARY DOOR: THE POWER OF THE SCHOOL LIBRARIAN IN AN EVOLVING INFORMATION LANDSCAPE

Donna Mignardi and Jennifer Sturge

ABSTRACT

Knowing your why is a powerful thing. As school librarians, an integral part of our mission is to ensure that students leave their K-12 education as information and media literate members of our society. In order for that to happen, students must also exit their K-12 years understanding how implicit and confirmation bias play a role in the way they view the world. That's part of the basis of our why:

School librarians are critical, necessary, and integral to ensuring we graduate students who are not only college and career ready but also have a deep understanding of how bias affects perception when it comes to being information and media literate.

School libraries are the epicenter of information and media literacy instruction. Because school librarians have the expertise and the background, they are a first line of defense in the broadening landscape of misinformation and a key player in combating fake news. Additionally, school librarians are uniquely poised to assist students in understanding bias – in particular confirmation and

Hope and a Future: Perspectives on the Impact that Librarians and Libraries Have on our World
Advances in Librarianship, Volume 48, 13–22
Copyright © 2021 by Emerald Publishing Limited
All rights of reproduction in any form reserved
ISSN: 0065-2830/doi:10.1108/S0065-283020210000048002

implicit biases that may affect the student's search for information. This chapter will address the power of the school librarian in an ever-evolving information landscape.

Keywords: Confirmation bias; digital citizenship; implicit bias; information literacy; school librarians; instruction

Everyone is entitled to his own opinion, but not to his own facts. (Moynihan, 2020, September 6)

In order to effectively address the why in this chapter, it is important to provide definitions for key terms:

Confirmation bias is the tendency that most humans have to interpret evidence as the confirmation of existing beliefs or theories. Essentially, confirmation bias is when a consumer of information seeks out and assigns more weight to theories or evidences that back up a claim or belief.

Implicit bias refers to attitudes or stereotypes that affect our decisions, understanding of the world, and our actions in an unconscious manner.

Media literacy is "the ability to access, analyze, evaluate, and create media in a variety of forms" (Center for Media Literacy, 2016). This definition has been expanded to also include media literacy as building "an understanding of the role of media in society as well as essential skills of inquiry and self-expression necessary for citizens of a democracy."

Information literacy is defined by the American Library Association (2018) as recognizing when information is needed, being able to locate, evaluate, and use information effectively.

By teaching information literacy with a focus on bias, school librarians prepare our students to be media literate, news literate, voter literate, and digital literate. Thus, we help to ensure that students have the knowhow to check their biases at the door. This chapter will explore ways in which to engage students with thinking about their own bias and exploring information literacy in order to encourage students to understand their own *why* when seeking out information.

CONFIRMATION BIAS

Let's begin with confirmation bias. We are certain there have been times when you have been having a seemingly innocent conversation with a colleague and all of a sudden, something comes rolling off their tongue that leaves your mouth hanging open in disbelief. Your first thought might be, "how could someone who works with me think *that*?" Pause for a second. There is probably some confirmation bias going on – on both sides!

Keep in mind that confirmation bias is the tendency that humans have to believe what they see and read in a way that fits into their personal beliefs. Both you and your colleague are most likely experiencing confirmation bias as confirmation bias impacts not only how you *gather* information, but also how you *interpret* the information gathered.

In a National Public Radio (NPR) interview, Michel Martin interviewed Johnathan Ellis, a professor of Philosophy at the University of California, Santa Cruz. Professor Ellis researches confirmation bias at the Center for Public Philosophy. During the interview, Professor Ellis mentioned something worth pointing out :

> Thucydides, an ancient Greek historian, wrote that it's a habit of human beings to use sovereign reason to thrust aside what they do not fancy. And what he was describing, and in fact what countless playwrights, philosophers and novelists have described ever since, are these human tendencies towards confirmation bias, rationalizations, self-deception. (Ellis, 2017)

What Professor Ellis is telling us is that confirmation bias is not a new idea or phenomenon. It dates back to the ancient Greeks and is part of human nature.

Why does checking our bias and being aware of confirmation bias matter? What makes teaching about confirmation bias and information literacy so difficult is that before we can truly instruct our students, we must realize how important our own perspectives and points of view are in determining how we go about our instruction. Our own upbringing, our racial, and our ethnic backgrounds play a role in how we receive messages from the media. As teacher, librarians we must understand how media messages are constructed and understand the techniques that the media uses to capture the attention of our students.

Our lessons and actions in the library must make students aware of their own bias. Students who are information literate understand that they will have confirmation bias and can take steps to check their bias as they interpret and synthesize information.

We want our students to be researchers and to understand the research process. Luhtala and Whiting (2018, pp. 21–22) outline that the purpose of research is to:

- Explore a concept.
- Formulate a line of inquiry out of initial discoveries.
- Deepen knowledge by investigating multiple perspectives.
- Document developing learning.
- Synthesize learning into an original idea.
- Articulate and publish that idea.
- Incorporate new learning into their knowledge base for reflection and future retrieval and consultation.

However, the authors also state that too many high school students finish their high school careers without "practicing and learning" (2018, p. 21) the steps to research and rely on their confirmation bias by approaching tasks already "knowing what they want to say" (Luhtala & Whiting, 2018, p. 21) and searching for information that supports their beliefs.

Because students often get their news from their social media feeds, they are insulated in algorithms that shape and filter what they see. Essentially, students are becoming entrenched in sealed media ecosystems also referred to as echo chambers. "Confronting this reality is a crucial component of teaching news literacy, which we define as the ability ... to discern credible information from raw information, opinion, misinformation and propaganda" (Miller, 2016, p. 276).

Our media landscape is changing so rapidly and drastically, librarians have begun to rethink strategies and teaching methods to meet students where they are and to best serve student needs. Just the fact that post-truth and fake news have been legitimized and highlighted by members of our own government and media underlines the importance and adds value to the importance of teaching about confirmation bias while teaching information literacy skills.

In order to check their confirmation bias, students need to be able to:

- Understand newsworthiness;
- Investigate sourcing and documentation; and
- Identify opinion, sponsored content, and reporting.

We can start by integrating lessons that teach explicitly about confirmation bias. Students need to understand what confirmation bias is and be aware of their own biases. Start students on the road to understanding with essential questions. These essential questions are great conversation starters for students at the secondary level:

- How can people have such different understandings of the facts of a situation?
- What is confirmation bias and how does it relate to the way we move through the world?

Using electronic resources and really digging into the research process is another way that school librarians can promote guided synthesis and analysis of issues. Frequently, school libraries subscribe to at least one database that has the ability to look at issues from a variety of viewpoints. Have students look at multiple viewpoints and choose to argue a viewpoint that is contradictory to the one they currently hold.

In 2015, *The New York Times* published an online piece by David Leonhardt to test problem-solving skills. In order to take the test, you must decipher a rule about a sequence of three numbers. The article states that the sequence 2, 4, 8 obeys the rule. At this point, the reader is challenged to enter number sequences into the boxes on the screen and test their ideas about the sequences. Once the reader feels they have tested enough sequences, they are able to type in their own theory describing the rule.

What is most intriguing about this exercise is exemplified in Leonhardt's observation that:

> most people start off with the incorrect assumption that since they are being asked to solve a problem, it must be a tricky problem. People do not want to hear the answer no; they don't want to be wrong. People prefer to hear an answer of yes. (Leonhardt, 2015)

This disappointment is a form of confirmation bias – people are more likely to believe the information that fits their pre-existing belief: "this puzzle must be hard if you want me to solve it."

Why spend two paragraphs talking about this 2015 article? It is a great way to introduce the idea of confirmation bias to high school students – it can sow the seed that sometimes you might think that you are right, you might be asking the right questions, but the answer may not fit neatly into your beliefs.

At the younger grades, working with students on understanding a simple research model can set up good habits for later on. One suggestion is to start in kindergarten with asking questions and modeling as a class how to go about finding the answers to the questions. As students progress through the elementary years, add more complex tasks and model researching across multiple resources.

Another incredibly important piece to this is ensuring that students understand how to cite their sources and leave elementary school with an understanding of what makes an authoritative, reliable, and credible source. There are a few mnemonics that can be used to assist students in evaluating their sources, if that is relevant in your situation such as the Currency, Relevance, Authority, Accuracy, Purpose test.

No matter what piece of the research process or which process you choose to follow, spending time directly instructing students to understand that there is confirmation bias is of the utmost importance.

IMPLICIT BIAS

> The single story creates stereotypes, and the problem with stereotypes is not that they are untrue, but that they are incomplete. They make one story become the only story. (Adichie, 2009)

At the beginning of this chapter, we addressed the definition of confirmation bias and implicit bias. We also shared our why. As we move into a discussion of implicit bias, revisiting our *why* seems relevant and worthy of a second look:

> School librarians are critical, necessary and integral to ensuring we graduate students who are not only college and career ready but also have a deep understanding of how bias affects perception when it comes to being information and media literate.

We have taken one look at the second part of our why – how confirmation bias affects perception. It's now time to dig into implicit bias. As Ms Adichie states in the above quote, having a single story creates stereotypes. It allows implicit bias to go unchecked. Understanding all of our stories is how we combat implicit bias. What makes the school librarian's job much more difficult when it comes to addressing implicit bias is that in many instances, teachers, students, parents, community members, and humans as a whole do not even realize that they walk around every day with implicit biases that are unconscious biases. We are unaware that we even own implicit biases. Implicit biases are ingrained into our conscious and unconscious selves from the world around us, from the media, from our social media echo-chambers, and are difficult to change.

Once you recognize your own bias, you can work to change that bias. As librarians, we need to ensure that our students understand that everyone has implicit bias. It does not make someone a bad person. It simply makes them human.

Before we can address how to recognize implicit bias with students, we need to teach teachers to recognize their own bias as well. One way to start to broach what can be a subject that some are uncomfortable talking about is to take an implicit bias test. The Harvard Implicit Bias test is one such test that will open the taker's eyes to many different biases. Another excellent implicit bias test to try is the one created at Yale, which helps to pinpoint and make the taker aware of their own perceptions. We believe that once you become more aware of your own biases, change can happen. A faculty who understands and recognizes that bias is a part of the human experience will be more prepared to address inequities in the classroom. It is when we do not take the time to recognize our own bias that we cannot do the work of educating our students.

> Teachers – and their implicit biases – can directly impact the opportunities afforded to students of color. Teachers make the first decisions about behavioral consequences that lead to referrals and suspensions. And they often serve as gatekeepers for gifted, honors, and Advanced Placement courses, deciding who to recommend for these tracks. (Schwartz, 2019)

It is important for school librarians to recognize their own implicit bias in order to serve students to the best of our ability. We want the library to be a safe, nurturing, and amazing environment for all. That means recognizing and overcoming preconceived ideas. Once we do that, we can then move on to work with our students.

Step one to teaching students is to define exactly what implicit bias is and to help them understand what their biases might be. A great way to start to introduce this topic with students is by using lessons from Teaching Tolerance. One of their essential questions when it relates to implicit bias is "How do the implicit biases we hold affect our interactions with the world?" (Teaching Tolerance, n.d.)

One of the best ways to demonstrate this is to utilize the New York Times Learning Network, where students can analyze photographs stripped of their headlines to test their literacy skills while thinking about any implicit biases they might hold. Activities like utilizing the New York Times Learning Network also give librarians opportunities to have honest conversations with students by digging into their reasoning for how they analyzed the picture. *The New York Times* has also put together a series of 25 short films that can be used in the classroom to spark conversation with students.

The Institute for Humane Education (n.d.) has many resources intended to help teachers assist their students in thinking deeply about implicit bias. Librarians can take advantage of resources that are available for teaching in this evolving information landscape. We encourage you to watch Verna Myer's powerful Ted Talk titled "How to Overcome our Biases? Walk Boldly Toward Them." It will spark conversation among your students and even your faculty.

Although internet resources are constantly changing, we feel strongly that the resources shared at the end of the chapter will be around for library and classroom use for a long time because they are so valuable.

INFORMATION LITERACY AND THE EVOLVING INFORMATION LANDSCAPE

Why is understanding bias so important to teaching students information literacy in an ever evolving information landscape?

In order to be productive, involved members of society, students must be able to distinguish fact from fiction, understand how media, news, and digital literacy play a large role in society. Students must exit our high schools understanding how bias plays a role in how we learn, what we do, and in our daily lives and the lives of others. Information literacy is educating our students to find answers to their questions and resources that provide valid information.

Teaching information literacy has changed in the past 20 years. Students have more information than ever before at their fingertips. Gone are the days of holding up a tabloid and a news trade publication and asking students to decide which is more authoritative, accurate, and current. It is no longer enough to teach location and evaluation of resources. Instead, information literacy should be taught as a dynamic experience and process. It cannot be complete until students truly understand the knowledge, skills, and attitudes of media, information, and technology content.

A recent survey by Common Sense Media and Survey Monkey found that teens today are getting the majority of their news online and are turning away from traditional media organizations. Instead, they are finding out about current events on social media and YouTube. They rely on social media influencers and celebrities for their current event information. Students are using Instagram, Facebook, and Twitter, with 50% getting their news from YouTube (Common Sense Media, 2019).

What is alarming about these statistics is that even though teens recognize that news from a news organization is more reliable, they still often use social media as their source. Nineteen percent of the teens surveyed reported that social media has made them more confused about the news. The other alarming piece of this information is that YouTube recommendations drive teen news consumption. This comes in the form of a "watch next" video in the sidebar (Common Sense Media, 2019).

How do we inspire students to think critically and be savvy consumers of information?

The focus for librarians should be on teaching the skills of information literacy to every student, every year while working on collaboration with their teachers. Teaching students the skills to unpack what they are seeing and reading will allow them to understand how their confirmation and implicit biases come into play and allow them to make informed decisions about what they see, hear, and read. Our role is to teach students about reliable sources of information and to understand how media messages are constructed, create an awareness of the techniques used by the media to capture our attention, and understand the reach and the impact of media.

- Teach students to search laterally.
- Show students how to search across multiple sites to verify information.
- Ensure that students understand the differences between sponsored content, blogs, opinion, and news.
- Practice unpacking articles of each type with students.

Encourage the use of fact-checking websites. Politifact (n.d.), Snopes (n.d.), and similar sites are great places to verify information. *The Washington Post* (n.d.) has a fact checker and Google does as well. Get students in the habit of questioning and verifying.

Make sure students are aware of and understand what social media echo chambers, filter bubbles, and algorithms do when it comes to what they see, view, and hear on websites.

Practice, practice, practice! There are a lot of amazing books available with ready-made lessons you can tailor to meet your students' needs. There are websites such as Checkology (n.d.) that offer great lessons on media bias and fake news. The Newesum's education department shares so many great teaching and learning resources – for free! Take advantage of them. KQED Education even has a micro-credential that librarians can earn in media literacy along with resources and ideas for sparking conversation and learning.

Librarians are powerful. We are information literacy warriors. We are social justice warriors. We have the knowledge and the know-how to check bias at our school library doors and provide students with the tools and the growth mindset that they will need to navigate life successfully and to live well and do great things!

Confirmation Bias Example: Gun Control

This is a controversial subject. It is also a great topic to show how confirmation bias affects our daily lives. Jane is in support of gun control. She finds herself looking for information in her social media feeds and in her magazines, internet searches, and newspapers that support limitations on guns. Joe is very much opposed to gun control. He believes that the second amendment should have no limitations and he seeks out information that supports his position. Everything that Jane and Joe find concerning gun control, they interpret to meet their own beliefs. Even if they were to read the same story, Jane would perceive the details differently than Joe.

Implicit Bias

Everyone possesses implicit bias – even those who are supposed to be impartial possess them (ex: judge).

Implicit biases can reinforce each other. They don't sit in isolation in our brains.

Implicit biases do not necessarily align with what we say we believe. In other words, we say one thing, but think another.

While in general, we tend to not hold implicit biases against our own group and our bias tend to favor our own group in society, we do sometimes hold implicit bias against those in our own group.

Because our brains are complex, we can unlearn implicit bias and we can change the way we think about bias.

REFERENCES

Adichie, C. N. (2009, July). *The danger of a single story* [Video file]. Retrieved from https://www.youtube. com/watch?v=D9Ihs241zeg

American Library Association. (2018). National school library standards for learners, school librarians, and school libraries. ALA Editions, an imprint of the American Library Association.

Awareness of Implicit Bias. (n.d.). Yale Poorvu Center for Teaching and Learning. Retrieved from https://poorvucenter.yale.edu/ImplicitBiasAwareness. Accessed on October 27, 2019.

Can People See What's Wrong with this Picture?. (2016, August 27). Video file. Retrieved from https://www.youtube.com/watch?time_continue=43&v=8vUi2RAuiO4

Center for Media Literacy. (2016). Retrieved from https://www.medialit.org/. Accessed on October 10, 2019.

Checkology. (n.d.). Retrieved from https://get.checkology.org/. Accessed on October 9, 2019.

Common Sense Media. (2019, August 12). New survey reveals teens get their news from social media and YouTube. Retrieved from https://www.commonsensemedia.org/ about-us/news/press-releases/new-survey-reveals-te ens-get-their-news-from-social-media-and-youtube. Accessed on October 20, 2019.

Ellis, J. (2017). Motivated Reasoning: A Philosopher on Confirmation Bias. *National Public Radio*, All Things Considered. Retrieved from https://www.npr.org/2017/01/28/512199352/confirmation-bias

Institute for Humane Education. (n.d.). Retrieved from https://humaneeducation.org/. Accessed on October 27, 2019.

Leonhardt, D. (2015, July 2). A quick puzzle to test your problem solving. *The New York Times*, The Upshot. Retrieved from https://www.nytimes.com/interactive/2015/07/03/upshot/a-quick-puzzle-to-test-your-problem-solving.html?_r=0

Luhtala, M., & Whiting, J. (2018). *News literacy: The keys to combating fake news*. Santa Barbara, CA: Libraries Unlimited.

Miller, A. (2016). Confronting Confirmation Bias: Giving Truth a Fighting Chance in the Information Age. *Social Education*, *80*(5), 276–279.

Moynihan, D. P. (2020, September 6). Wikipedia. Retrieved from https://en.wikipedia.org/wiki/Daniel _Patrick_Moynihan#:~:text=%22Everyone%20is%20entitled%20to%20his,but%20not%20 his%20own%20facts.%22. Accessed on October 9, 2020.

Schwartz, S. (2019). Next step in diversity training: Teachers learn to face their unconscious biases. *Education Week*, *38*(33). Retrieved from Gale Academic OneFile database. Retrieved from https://www.edweek.org/leadership/next-step-in-diversity-trainingteachers-learn-to-face-their-unconscious-biases/2019/05.

Snopes (n.d.). The definitive fact checking site and reference page. *Snopes.com*. Retrieved from https://www.snopes.com/. Accessed on October 27, 2019.

Teaching Tolerance. (n.d.). Retrieved from http://www.tolerance.org. Accessed on October 26, 2019.

The Washington Post. (n.d.). Fact checker. Retrieved from h ttps://www.washingtonpost.com/news/fact-checker/. Accessed on October 27, 2019.

FURTHER READING

De Abreu, B. S. (2019). *Teaching media literacy* (2nd ed.). Chicago, IL: ALA Neal-Schuman.

Facing History. (n.d.). Confirmation and other biases. Retrieved from https://www.facinghi story.org/resource-library/facing-ferguson-news-literacy-digital-age/confirmation-and-other-biases. Accessed on October 27, 2019.

Fact Check Tools. (n.d.). Google fact check tools: Fact check explorer. Retrieved from https://toolbox.google.com/factcheck/about. Accessed on October 27, 2019.

Gold, J. (2017, March 8). Teaching students about confirmation bias. *Teaching Tolerance*. Retrieved from https://www.tolerance.org/ magazine/teaching-students-about-confirmation-bias

Gonchar, M. (2017, March 15). 25 mini-films for exploring race, bias and identity with students. *The New York Times*, Film Club. Retrieved from https://www.nytimes.com/2017/03/15/learning/lesson-plans/25-mini-films-for-e xploring-race-bias-and-identity-with-students.html

Green, M., & Roberson, R. (2017, May 9). Quiz: How good are you at detecting bias? (with lesson plan). *KQED*. Retrieved from https://www.kqed.org/lowdown/26829/quiz-how-good-are-you-at-detecting-bias-with-lesson-plan. Accessed on October 27, 2019.

LaGarde, J., & Hudgins, D. (2018). *Fact vs fiction: Teaching critical thinking skills in the age of fake news*. Portland, OR: International Society for Technology in Education.

Media Literacy Educator Certification. (n.d.). Public broadcasting service. *KQED*. Retrieved from https://edu-landing.kqed.org/certification/. Accessed on October 25, 2019.

Motivated Reasoning. (n.d.). Motivated reasoning: A philosopher on confirmation bias [Radio episode]. *All things considered*. Retrieved from https:// www.npr.org/2017/01/28/512199352/confirmation-bias

MTV's Look Different. (n.d.). Retrieved from http://www.lookdifferent.org/. Accessed on October 27, 2019.

Myers, V. (2016, November). *How to overcome our biases? Walk boldly toward them* [Video file]. Retrieved from https://www.ted.com/talks/verna_myers_how_to_overc ome_our_biases_walk_boldly_toward_them?language=en

NewseumEd. (n.d.). Retrieved from https://newseumed.org/. Accessed on October 11, 2019.

PolitiFact. (n.d.). Fact checking US politics. *PolitiFact*. Retrieved from http://www.politifact.com. Accessed on October 27, 2019.

Project Implicit. (n.d.). Harvard University project implicit. Retrieved from https://implicit.harvard. edu/implicit/index.jsp. Accessed on October 27, 2019.

The New York Times. (2019, October 21). What's going on in this picture. *The New York Times*. Retrieved from https://www.nytimes. com/column/learning-whats-going-on-in-this-picture

We Need Diverse Books. (n.d.). Retrieved from https://diversebooks.org/. Accessed on October 27, 2019.

CHAPTER 3

THE PATH TO THE IVY LEAGUE LEADS STRAIGHT THROUGH THE PUBLIC LIBRARY

Aryssa Damron

ABSTRACT

With the college admissions process under the microscope after allegations of bribery, fraud, and other malfeasance, it is even more imperative for public libraries to play a role in helping students reach their fullest potential. From collection development to programming to community partnerships, the public library has a critical role to play in the college admissions process, especially in low-income communities. In a society where many people feel that they are at a disadvantage applying to elite schools already, the public library can offer a path forward and a path of hope.

Keywords: College admissions; public library; teen programming; test preparation; Ivy League; youth services

INTRODUCTION

While the media focuses on high-profile celebrity admissions scandals and the rising price of tuition, it is easy to forget the kids who pay for school with financial aid and Pell Grants, who check out their Scholastic Aptitude Test (SAT) tutors for three weeks at a time, who rely on Lynda and Universal Class and DuoLingo to get into the school of their dreams. Public libraries have an ever-evolving

Hope and a Future: Perspectives on the Impact that Librarians and Libraries Have on our World
Advances in Librarianship, Volume 48, 23–31
ISSN: 0065-2830/doi:10.1108/S0065-283020210000048003

role in modern society, but an often overlooked service population is the teens and young adults (YAs) applying to college and navigating the process with the resources available at local branches. From promoting lifelong literacy to stocking reliable test prep resources, public libraries can help shape the future of college admissions and create a more equitable process for their patrons.

FROM RURAL KENTUCKY TO YALE

When I walked onto the campus of Yale University in the fall of 2014, I was stepping somewhere that was not intended for people like me – people from rural areas, from low-income households, and from single parent homes. The path to get here was not laid out for me by family members or college counselors or SAT tutors; but I got there nonetheless, because I took the path through my local public library, and that made all the difference.

The role the public library played in my journey from rural Kentucky to the graduation ceremony of Yale University cannot be understated, but I am also not the only individual to take this path. It was well-worn when I trod it, with highlighted test prep materials and essay books and a special shelf of scholarship applications in the teen section of the public library I had frequented since birth. The library not only taught me the importance of literacy but by engaging my young mind with new, exciting programs and an ever-growing collection it encouraged me to keep coming back well into my teen years, when the library became an integral part of my college application process.

I grew up in a single-parent home with very active grandparents who encouraged a lifelong love of reading and never minded running me to the library several times a week. It helped that though my local library was small, it was mighty, and had a good selection of books for all ages. As I aged, the library also had a teen council and teen programming that kept me coming back even when I wasn't checking out a new book. When I entered high school, I would spend an hour in the nonfiction stacks, running my fingers across spines, and looking for something new to learn. When I finally got it into my head that I was going to go to a good college, I spent so much time staring at the 378 section that to this day I think I could recreate it for you in my mind. There were American College Test (ACT) prep books, study books for all the Advanced Placement (AP) courses I could ever want, books about writing college admissions essays and getting financial aid, and thick book after thick book detailing every four-year-college in the United States – their admissions processes and majors offered.

I would check these books out by the armload, hauling them into the car and spending night after night at the kitchen table, exploring a new university or deciding on a new major as the fancy struck. This was before college admissions was even real to me – long before I created my Common Application account, before I started exploring things I actually might write about in my admissions essays. This was a free way to explore my dreams and help me figure out which ones disappeared when I came across a better one and which ones stayed with me. I worked through every single ACT practice book on the shelves, checking each out for three weeks at a time. After a while, I started to see patterns, to pick up clues, and my score climbed and climbed with each practice test.

When I began actively applying to colleges, the 378 selection of my local public library was invaluable. I routinely cleaned out entire shelves. I relied on those ACT prep books – in multiples – and books about essay writing and applying for scholarships. I relied on the library's fax machine to send off paperwork (this was before scanners really took off) and sometimes the library's computers – though I now see how lucky I was that my house was never without a computer and internet access. Other patrons weren't as lucky and would spend entire afternoons at the library computer stations, typing away on their essays.

I was not cognizant at the time how lucky I was. I thought I was at the bottom of the pack in the race toward Ivy League admissions. I thought I was scraping by, making do, and in a way, I was. It wasn't until I was at the college of my dreams, Yale, that I realized I was surrounded by people who had SAT tutors and bought ACT prep classes online and hired people to read their essays. Not everyone was like that, but there were enough to encourage my own reflection upon my path to Yale. It wasn't supposed to be that path, I realized, but I had cleared the thicket and forged ahead using the tools provided to me by my local public library.

Now, working in a public library, I am a strong advocate for the curation of a great collection and want to show just how instrumental public libraries are in the college admissions process for so many. It's not just about teaching kids to love books either, it's about providing the space and the collection for continued growth – both independently and with guidance.

LITERACY SHAPES LIFELONG LEARNING

The college admissions process doesn't begin by making an account on the Common Application website or opening your mailbox to a deluge of prospective student packets. It begins at story time and teen council and summer reading demonstrations with NASA spacesuits. While a lot goes into college admissions and college readiness, an often-overlooked factor is the role of lifelong literacy (US News, 2014).

Teens won't know to rely on the library during the college admissions process if they have come to rely on the library during their formative years (Pew Research Center, 2014). It is a process to reroute the brain from seeking out picture books and DVDs of beloved cartoons to searching databases for test prep materials and signing onto the free computers to fill out your Free Application for Federal Student Aid (FAFSA). It is a process that can be done, but a library system first must devote themselves to lifelong literacy.

Childhood literacy is an easy project to sell. You want to teach children to read, you want to encourage them to read at higher and higher levels, you want to send free books to children under five, or partner with elementary school classrooms to promote popular books. However, this sort of gung-ho activism often tapers off once students enter middle and high school.

There are a couple ways to continue the promotion of literacy into the teen years and up through the college admissions process. One of those is organizing teen-centric programming that isn't necessarily related to reading but gets teens into the building. At my current branch, it's harder to keep the teens out than to keep them in, but we are still searching for ways to actively engage with these teens in programming that both interests them and serves them. Some branches organize video game nights, other poetry slams, and book clubs. The needs for each branch will differ according to the teens you serve, but what is important is having something for the teens that make them feel like the library is their home and a place they can come to. For us, this means having a teen and children's section on a separate floor so while we'd still like them not to yell and shout, the need for silence is not pushed upon them and therefore discouraging to their interactions. Some libraries offer free meals during the summer and after school snacks to attract young patrons, especially those who are best served by this free public resource.

Another aspect of the library that will result in more engagement during the college application process is having a YA fiction section that reflects the interests and needs of the readers. The YA section should be well stocked with both the classics and the popular adaptations (*The Hate U Give, Five Feet Apart*, etc.) but also with new and diverse books that serve as mirrors and windows for the teens that will be browsing those shelves. This includes having a plentiful graphic novel and comic book section and recognizing those as valid forms of reading that will attract many YA readers that might otherwise not be selecting books from the shelves.

TEST PREP AND THE VIRTUE OF WEEDING

As a graduate student in library science, I was tasked with a fictitious weeding project for a collection development class. The task was to pick a single branch of a library (easier for me, with 26 options nearby, than some of my classmates) and select approximately 20 titles to be weeded from the collection and replacements for each of them. We were to focus on one particular section: poetry or YA fantasy or books about computers, et cetera. I chose the college prep section, particularly the 378s, of my local branch. As a former book hoarder that became the person who gives away her finished book to strangers on the train, I had come to appreciate the idea of weeding, but only after exploring this relatively newly renovated library's 378 collection did I realize that weeding is a civic necessity in public libraries (McElfresh, 2017).

Having done my graduate studies directly after undergraduate, I was approximately five years out of my college application stage when I completed the weeding project. Yet, in those five years, a lot has changed about college admissions. Photoshop aside, the way the SAT is scored changed while I was in college, and the Common App became increasingly common (Princeton Review, n.d.). Another similar website, The Coalition App, was launched while I was picking out my first-year class schedule. If these major changes could occur in such a short period of time, there is clearly a need for a critical eye on the college prep collection of each library to ensure that the materials being offered to patrons are accurate and helpful instead of misleading and particularly harmful. It is not acceptable to leave out of date and inaccurate material for low-income patrons while knowing that their more affluent peers are getting a leg up with up-to-date and correct information.

While one might assume that a student registering for the SAT in fall 2019 and studying from a book from 2013 would do the research to determine the change in testing standards and scoring, that is simply not always the case. Especially for low-income students and students without adequate digital resources, test prep books at the library might be their only source of information on tests like the SAST, ACT, Armed Services Vocational Aptitude Battery (ASVAB), Preliminary SAT (PSAT), and General Education Development (GED). It is therefore a civic responsibility of public libraries to ensure that the materials they are offering are not setting their patrons up for failure. It is safer to assume that this one book is their only source of knowledge on the subject than to assume they will do a full-fledged research project on the new SAT scoring guidelines.

Similarly, public libraries should keep abreast of the general college information materials they are offering. At the library I studied for this particular weeding project, I discovered college application guidelines written before online applications existed (and therefore very outdated) along with books on getting into Harvard published when I was in elementary school. While some aspects of the college admissions process will always remain, the rapid changes brought about by technology, devotion to diversification, and overall cultural expectations have created a publishing boom of college prep books that libraries can purchase to keep their collection more up-to-date (Jacob, O'Brien, & Reid, 2014).

Other books that should appear, in an up-to-date version, in library collections include books about the FAFSA and financial aid options for students as well as unbiased books that talk about student loans. Books published by agencies that oversee those loans are not always the most reliable when it comes to helping students pay for college without taking on burdensome debt. Many publishers also put out big books, hundreds of pages long, on national and local scholarships.

If money is an issue, and it always seems to be in public libraries, increased awareness of the area can aid collection development. For example, in the Kentucky town I grew up in, the ACT was offered frequently and you had to drive an hour to take the SAT. Therefore, the library focused on acquiring ACT materials in larger quantities than SAT materials. Similarly, they acquired fewer preparation materials for AP courses not offered at the local high schools, such as human geography and Japanese. By doing a bit of research, talking to local partners, and staying tuned into the needs of the teens of the area, librarians are able to put limited funds where they will do the most good without necessarily restricting the collection from continued growth.

While these are ways the public library's collection can support college-bound students, there are also potential programs, both passive and active, that can turn the library into a path-carver for patrons.

PASSIVE PROGRAMMING

Passive programming allows public libraries to ensure they are engaging with patrons and giving them opportunities to use the library's resources without carving out regular time or insisting upon one meeting time or space for engagement. Especially for teens and YAs, passive programming allows them to engage at their own leisure and learn about library resources without being lectured at. After spending eight hours in a classroom, few teens want to come to the public library and experience a similar situation. Rather, they want the freedom to explore and engage with their own interests. That presents a unique opportunity for public libraries to organize passive ways to promote college prep materials and related library resources.

The first passive activity that public libraries should engage in is smart displays of college preparation and testing related materials. While most libraries relegate the 378s to general nonfiction, others choose to include at least some of those materials in the teen section or displayed on their own to accommodate potential information seekers who may not otherwise be in the general nonfiction section. This is especially critical for libraries that have different floors for children/teens and general adults. If teens enter the library every day and head upstairs but the test prep materials are downstairs, how are they supposed to discover them?

Especially during the late fall semester, it may behoove public libraries to publicly display these materials in a way that makes them accessible to all patrons visiting the library – including applicants and their parents. Perhaps they could be displayed near the check-out section, or adjacent to regularly used public computers. Any active programming related to college applications, as discussed in the next section, should also feature some pulled materials in the room for interested parties to check out.

Another passive way to promote library resources related to the college application and admissions process is by creating to-go materials on what the library offers. For example, a display of digital resource materials might include a flyer specifically on the resources that applicants can utilize through the library – Khan Academy, databases, Tutor.com, etc.

Bookmarks provide a great chance to give teens the information they may not even know they need. With each checkout, for example, a teen could receive a bookmark about these resources offered by the library or created by a partner about relevant details and deadlines, such as upcoming ACT dates. Partners and local colleges will also likely provide, eagerly and for free, resources that libraries can display related to their admissions processes. While public libraries should not promote one local college over another, having a dedicated "local colleges" flyer section in the teen session may attract potential applicants and raise an interest in teens that frequent the library but may not be actively thinking about college applications.

Another passive way to engage teen patrons and other potential college applicants with library resources is to be a repository for local scholarship applications to be displayed, advertised, and promoted. A teen section could feature copies of scholarship applications for students to pick up and fill out, though ultimately the burden of return rests with the student and that scholarship committee. However, because there are often so many diverse local groups offering these scholarships, places like public libraries and school libraries provide a potential nexus point for interested parties. While most school libraries or guidance counselors likely do promote these local scholarships, displays at a public library may also attract the parents and guardians of these applicants, who may have a larger stake in promoting the need for scholarships.

ACTIVE PROGRAMMING

Active programming allows public library professionals to engage in hands-on experiences with patrons and address their needs directly. Active programming can occur on a routine basis, perhaps weekly or monthly, or even just once a year, and gives a dedicated time and space to devote to a particular activity. Dedicating active programming to a topic shows that you value it that it holds a place in your library's mission.

At the public library where I work, there are only four computers designated for teen use, and they are often occupied with teens watching music videos and playing games. Even teens that come specifically to use the computers for home-work, since many households in our neighborhood do not have personal comput-ers, have to wait awhile for a seat.

Here in Washington, DC, I am organizing SAT Test Prep Sessions in our public library computer lab that not only provides a way to showcase digital resources, specifically the Teaching and Education Research Center (TERC), but also makes use of our newly renovated computer lab. The computer lab, which seats 10, is reserved solely for the classes taught by library staff – such as email basics, Microsoft Suite, Jasperactive testing, etc. These classes are primarily geared toward adults and seniors. Since the teen area only has four available com-puters, which are often used for gaming and social networking, opening the com-puter lab for organized SAT test prep sessions makes sense for our community. In promoting the program, I reached out to nearby schools to advertise and made it clear that each session – one each week – would focus on a particular section of the exam. I then prepared instructions sheets so that attendees could recreate the test prep experience at home, outside of our regularly scheduled program-ming. Associated materials – including SAT prep books, algebra books, guides for vocabulary – are also made available during the program, which takes place each Tuesday after school.

In deciding how to organize such an event, I took note of the upcoming SAT date and spoke to local guidance counselors who oversee the school-wide SAT testing day (Princeton Review, n.d.). Other areas may have more success with ACT test prep sessions. The TERC is easy and free to use via our library and has practice sessions for a variety of tests. If the SAT sessions are successful, we hope to offer more testing for college prep and readiness exams. School libraries may have great success organizing practice test sessions for the AP courses taught in their school, which will vary.

Another way, libraries can actively program for the college application crowd is by hosting FAFSA workshop (ELA Area Public Library, n.d.). Either internally or externally hosted, this is a great opportunity to showcase library resources for both the applicants and their parents, who will likely be highly involved in that aspect of the process. Learning how to fill out the FAFSA and having a designated time and space for that is critical, especially for students relying heavily on the public library during the process. Even nonacademic librarians can learn about the FAFSA and how it works, and while staff should not be expected to handle sensitive tax information, they can be on hand to answer tech-related questions and provide general guidance and encouragement on the process (Brooklyn Public Library, 2019). While teens, as opposed to older patrons, are less likely to need assistance sending an email or saving a file, they may not know how to pull their parents tax information from the Internal Revenue Service (IRS) or convert something to a PDF for upload, so staff should be ready to assist with this sort of thing. For something like this, it's also possible to partner with a local financial aid counselor who could go into specifics or show a presentation provided by the FAFSA itself.

Other active programming ideas include college fairs with local universities and community colleges, essay writing workshops, virtual college visits, practice interviews, and more. The key is to know your area and take advantage of the relationships you can form.

These sorts of active programming are just as much about providing a space and opportunity as the knowledge, though any staff overseeing these programs should have a baseline knowledge of the procedures of modern college applications, what local schools want out of applicants (which tests, deadlines, etc.) as well as strong digital literacy skills.

POTENTIAL FOR PARTNERSHIPS

Public libraries are often called upon to go above and beyond their expertise and their resources, and one way to accomplish this without sacrificing well-intentioned staff members is to seek out partnerships.

Most major cities will have groups devoted to college admissions that would be happy to help. Local universities are always eager to send out representatives to talk about admissions to their school in particular. For example, here in Washington, DC, presentations on college admissions do focus on the local schools and those schools often provide resources about their application process, fee waivers, informational packets, etc., to libraries looking to partner with them in formal or informal ways. Including partnerships with both four-year universities and community colleges and vocational schools ensures that all patrons will be able to find something that suits the path they envision for themselves without necessarily being closed off to other options.

Growing up in rural Kentucky, if I had picked a school out of only what my school guidance counselor talked about, I would have at most ended up an hour and a half from home. Instead, I relied on the library which, while forming these partnerships, also encouraged my exploration of schools far away both online and in their printed resources. Some small town libraries even host digital college fairs for schools like Yale, Harvard, Duke, and Stanford that may want to attract students from these areas but not have a representative nearby. Thanks to the success of teleconferencing software like Zoom and Skype, these visits are increasingly feasible for small town libraries seeking to have the ideas of an individual, college, or agency represented within their branch. The costs are low and the ability to serve is high.

Other potential partners in the college admissions process include alumni in the area who are willing to talk about their experience with both admissions and actual college life. Admissions are such a daunting process to so many that the actual years spent in college are forgotten about until they arise. These sorts of informal partnerships, with patrons of the past offering insight to patrons of the present, can be a comfort for many and provide insight into the current processes that older library professionals may miss.

CONCLUSION

As public libraries are called on to fill even more gaps in society and step up to help, it is critical that the college admissions process and its ability to change the life of patrons is kept in mind. While many will choose not to pursue higher education, others will want the opportunity and the public library is in a unique position to provide valuable resources on the topic and shape lives for years to come. For me, the college admissions process is the result of a lifelong love of learning and literacy that was instilled in me at story times and teen council meetings. Somewhere like Yale would have been out of reach if not for the public library. So while public libraries are stepping up to help the homeless, and the hungry, and infants, and senior citizens, let us not forget the teens and YAs who come into their neighborhood branch in search of a way to level the ever-changing playing field of college admissions.

REFERENCES

Brooklyn Public Library. (2019, April 10). The future is yours: FAFSA workshop. Retrieved from https://www.bklynlibrary.org/calendar/future-yours-fafsa-brownsville-library-20190327. Accessed on October 1, 2019.

ELA Area Public Library. (n.d.). FAFSA completion workshop. Retrieved from https://www.eapl.org/events/fafsa-completion-workshop. Accessed on September 5, 2019.

Jacob, M., O'Brien, S., & Reid, B. (2014). Weeding the collection: Perspectives from three public librarians. In B. Albitz (Ed.), *Rethinking collection development and management* (pp. 77–88). Santa Barbara, CA: Libraries Unlimited.

McElfresh, L. (2017). Crash course in weeding library collections. *Technicalities, 37*(6), 18–20. Retrieved from https://search-proquest-com.ezproxy.uky.edu/docview/2033275024?accountid=11836&rfr_id=info%3Axri%2Fsid%3Aprimo. Accessed on September 19, 2019.

Pew Research Center. (2014, September 10). Younger Americans and public libraries. Retrieved from http://www.pewinternet.org/2014/09/10/younger-americans-and-public-libraries. Accessed on October 8, 2019.

Princeton Review. (n.d.). The new SAT. We're on it. Retrieved from https://www.princetonreview.com/college/sat-changes. Accessed on October 1, 2019.

US News. (2014, September 22). Public libraries offer more than just books to teens. Retrieved from https://www.usnews.com/education/blogs/high-school-notes/2014/09/22/public-libraries-offer-more-than-just-books-to-teens. Accessed on October 3, 2019.

SECTION 2

DIVERSE AND INCLUSIVE

CHAPTER 4

MOVING BEYOND BUZZWORDS: BELONGING IN LIBRARY COLLECTIONS

Paolo P. Gujilde

ABSTRACT

The changing demographics of the United States are reflected in the changing faces in universities and colleges across the nation. However, universities and colleges, including academic libraries, are still reacting as opposed to being proactive to these changes in their campuses. Academic libraries especially in the area of library resources are still grappling with the question of "How can we diversify our library collections?" In this chapter, the author examines the idea that one of the ways to reflect demographics on campus is for academic libraries to explore the concept of "belongingness" – the idea that students are seeing themselves on campus. This examination of belongingness hopes to answer the lack of representation of minority students in library collections through identifying gaps in the collection and acquiring diverse books and other resources. For minority students to see themselves in higher education institutions, academic libraries need to be proactive in helping students "belong" on campus.

Keywords: Libraries; belonging; diversity; library collections; minority students; collection development

Hope and a Future: Perspectives on the Impact that Librarians and Libraries Have on our World
Advances in Librarianship, Volume 48, 35–41
ISSN: 0065-2830/doi:10.1108/S0065-283020210000048004

INTRODUCTION

Diversity in libraries can be argued as one the challenges libraries are facing today and the future. Yet, diversity is still much more of concept rather than the reality. The need for diversity in academic libraries especially within library services and library collections is much more significant today. The changing demographics are pushing academic libraries to provide services and resources that capture the mold of a college campus. Academic libraries and its services play an important role in the growth and success of students in higher education. These services provide avenues for college students, especially minority college students to feel that they "belong" on-campus and that they are represented.

The growth of minority student enrollments and changing college student population statistics are reflections of the current and future trends of shifts in population of the United States of America. The National Center for Education Statistics released that Hispanics had a growth of 141% in college enrollment (Krogstad & Fry, 2014). The general population of the United States since 2000 is showing an upward trend in minority populations of Hispanic descent and Asian descent (Passel, Cohn, & Lopez, 2011; Pew Research Center, 2012). In 2010, the general US census revealed a 43% increase of Latino population (Passel et al., 2011). Additionally, immigrants from Asian nations such as China, the Philippines, and India increased 36% compared to 31% of immigrants from Latin American countries (Pew Research Center, 2012). With the shift in the general population, college and university student population is also changing. These current and future trends in student populations will have an effect on the future of libraries especially on library services and collections.

As our population grows and our demographic changes, libraries need to react and eventually prepare itself to be a reflection of our communities and campuses. In this chapter, we will explore the concept of "belonging" and the simple ideas we can implement to guide our work in diversifying library collections and to move beyond the buzzwords.

WHAT IS "BELONGING"?

Belonging is not a new concept. In fact, Maslow (1943) identified "love and belong-ingness" as one of the basic needs that motivate humans in his theory of human motivation. It is a factor in how, we, as humans feel about our surroundings and feel about how we motivate ourselves every day. Other researchers affirmed and amplified Maslow's ideas on belongingness. For example, Baumeister and Leary (1995) suggested that "the human being is naturally driven toward establishing and sustaining belongingness" (p. 499). Their work on the "need to belong" is conceptualized in two main features of it: (1) "people need frequent personal contacts or interactions with other person" and (2) "people need to perceive that there is an interpersonal bond or relationship marked stability, affective concern, and continuation into the foreseeable future" (Baumeister & Leary, 1995, p. 500). The impact of belongingness or in this case, the need to belong, emphasized the relationship between an individual to another or a person to group. Affiliation to a group is an act of belongingness.

Strayhorn (2019) applied concepts of belongingness in the realm of college students and presented it as "sense of belonging" since the mid-2000s. Sense of belonging is "framed as a basic human need and motivation, sufficient to influence behavior" (Strayhorn, 2019, p. 54). This is, in fact, similar sentiments and definitions as defined by Maslow (1943) and Baumeister and Leary (1995). In addition, Strayhorn (2019), through the lens of college students, further defined sense of belonging as:

> students' perceived social support on campus, a feeling or sensation of connectedness, the experience of mattering or feeling cared about, accepted, respected, valued by, and important to the group (e.g. campus community) or others on campus (e.g. faculty, peers). (p. 54)

Beyond the definitions and framing of belongingness, studies related to belonging of college students focused on nonimmigrant and immigrant students, minority students, freshman students, and students with disabilities (Bodaghi & Zainab, 2013; Freeman, Anderman, & Jensen, 2007; Hachey & McCallen, 2018; Hurtado & Carter, 1997). For example, Hachey and McCallen (2018) study that belonging differs heavily between nonimmigrant and immigrant students in which nonimmigrant students have more of a sense of belonging than immigrant students. These studies reflect the different point of view of many individuals experiencing the basic needs of belonging within an environment.

In libraries, Bodaghi and Zainab (2013) studied the sense of belonging of visually impaired students within libraries. In this study, carrels provided a sense of belonging to students in the library. Library space as a service by the library enhances the feeling of belonging for students. At Pennsylvania State University, a case study on international students' sense of belonging in libraries provided information on international undergraduate students' perspective of belonging in the library (Gant, Amsberry, Su, Munip, & Borrelli, 2019). For instance, participants of the focus group appreciated the library collections such as the "multicultural collections, exhibits, and international newspapers" as they reflected the home countries of the international undergraduate students (Gant et al., 2019).

DIVERSITY IN LIBRARY COLLECTIONS

There are many challenges affecting diversity in library collections: from lack of support across different levels of the organization to lack of awareness to the needs of the students. However, one of the challenges in diversifying library collections is budget or the allocation of funds to acquire diverse library materials. Library collection development is the process of selecting and acquiring library resources to support the curriculum as well as to provide resources for students, faculty, staff, and other stakeholders. Collection development includes but not limited to purchasing books, subscribing to journals and databases, and compiling resources for the library. Funding for collection development depends heavily on the type of institution and the mission of the library. For example, Research

1 universities have a much higher funding for collection development as opposed to a regional comprehensive university or a community college. In this instance, funding can become an issue especially if there is not much to distribute to various acquisition of materials for academic units.

Hence, collection development in academic libraries specifically for diversity purposes is sometimes placed near the bottom of acquisition priorities. However, colleges and universities are moving forward with ideas and plans to provide diverse library collections. Though, again, the mission of the library and the institution matters, diverse library collections take shape in many different areas of the library. Some may not be about books or library resources but they are statements that assure library stakeholders of its diversity commitment.

Outside of libraries, new initiatives and programs related to diversity in libraries and diversifying library collections are much more prominent in the last decade. These initiatives are established to combat, in some cases, biases with diverse themes in literature and/or biases on the quality of literature by authors of color. Thus, organizations such as We Need Diverse Books (WNDB), for example, exist. WNDB, a nationally recognized grassroots organization that aims to "produce and promote literature that reflects and honors the lives of all young people," is helping grow diversity in library collections (We Need Diverse Books, n.d.)

The American Library Association (ALA) has been invested in equity, diversity, and inclusion (EDI) initiatives. For example, ALA members have been asked to provide feedback on the Library Bill of Rights interpretation related to library collections. Conferences and meetings, from general library conferences to more specific conferences on library collections and acquisitions, have presented programs and sessions related to diverse library collections. In addition, ALA Midwinter 2019 saw the expansion of the Youth Media Awards with the announcements of literature award winners from the Asian Pacific American Librarians Association (APALA) and others. With that said, it is safe to say that EDI and diverse library collections are the buzzwords.

In the last few years, we have been discussing and implementing EDI initiatives. Some implementations have succeeded and some not so much. To move beyond buzzwords, we must first have a common understanding of the buzzwords. With this, I look into the definitions by ALA, established in the last few years (American Library Association, n.d.b):

- Equity – "means increasing diversity by ameliorating conditions of disadvantage groups."
- Diversity – "can be defined as the sum of the ways that are both alike and different."
- Inclusion – "means an environment in which all individuals are treated fairly and respectfully ... have equal access to resources and opportunities ...."

The common language and definitions bring us to a common understanding on what EDI is and what it holds for the future of libraries.

In addition to the definitions, American Library Association's (n.d.a) Library Bill of Rights emphasizes two important aspects of diversity in library collections: (1) Books and other materials should be provided to patrons without biases and (2) Libraries should provide different points of view. The Library Bill of Rights guides some of the responsibilities of libraries and librarians in providing diverse library collections. Furthermore, ALA's ethical standards highlight the ethical responsibility of which libraries and librarians provide equitable and unbiased library resources American Library Association (n.d.c).

"BELONGING" AND LIBRARIES: HOW DO WE MOVE BEYOND BUZZWORDS?

Belonging is a concept associated with behavior and motivation and often relates to connectedness from one human being to another human being or from a human being to a group. However, I want this belongingness to include human being's connectedness to library collections. Our students and our patrons should see themselves through the resources that we select to be added to the library.

So, how can we make our library collections belong to our students and our patrons? How can we make a difference through our work? From selection to evaluation, it is important to build beyond buzzwords of diverse library collections. Below are some recommendations, simple ideas that, hopefully, guide the way we work with library collections:

1. Scanning our library collections – An environmental scan of our library collections helps in identifying gaps and areas of opportunities. This is where we should be asking questions about visibility and representation of students in the collections.
2. Awareness of personal biases – One of the tenets and responsibilities of librarians is to be cognizant of personal biases as we serve our patrons and our communities. Biases, whether explicit or implicit, impacts the way we serve our communities, and this, sometimes, manifests in our selections and acquisitions of library collections.
3. Creating simple diversity statements – Most of us are familiar with diversity statements in libraries especially as we try to diversify our library collections. However, as we write these statements, we tend to bring grandiose ideas and concepts which eventually become lost during implementation. Simple diversity statements could help ease, sometimes difficult, the process of strategic collection development. For example, instead of a blanket statement on diversity, they provide attainable acquisitions of ALA's ethnic affiliates' book awards selections. In addition, a diversity statement is *just* a statement without a budgetary line. So, I encourage organizations to go beyond statements and include budget allocation to acquire diverse library materials.
4. Awareness of ethnic affiliates and acquiring their book award winners – This is one of the simplest and attainable start in acquiring diverse library collections. Every librarian and information professional should be aware of the work of the ethnic affiliates and its literature awards. The Black Caucus of the American Library Association, American Indian Library Association,

Asian Pacific American Librarians Association, Chinese American Librarians Association, REFORMA: The National Association to Promote Library and Information Services to Latinos and the Spanish Speaking. Each of these ALA ethnic affiliates advocates for underserved and underrepresented librarians and communities. In addition, each of these groups selects and awards books, annually or biannually.

5. Acquiring materials by authors of color – As librarians, we have the privilege to select materials for our patrons and our communities. With this, we have the opportunity and the "power" to select books and other resources by authors of color. This process could be as simple as buying a book to be added to the library collection. Acquiring diverse library collection needs to be intentional and deliberate as we have the capability to do so.

6. Reinforcing library collections with library programming/services – Library programming is a great way to enhance library collections and a good way to introduce patrons to the library collections. Exhibits highlighting works by authors of color are just an example on how we move beyond buzzwords. Some libraries create book clubs and story times dedicated to books published in a language other than English.

7. Engaging with public libraries and other partners – Public libraries are great examples of reflecting their changing demographics. In some areas, highly diverse communities have specific collections dedicated to communities within the larger community. Student organizations are also great partners in getting insight into the needs and wants of the students.

These are not groundbreaking ideas or recommendations; however, these are ideas that need to be emphasized as some of us grapple with how we connect our communities to our libraries especially in colleges and universities. Diversifying library collections and moving beyond the buzzwords are about visibility and representation of marginalized and underrepresented members of the society and members of our campuses.

CONCLUSION

The changing demographics drive our motivation in libraries. They guide us to meet the needs of our students and our patrons. The current state of library collections is representations of outdated collection development policies, and for the most part, it is no longer reflections of the curriculum and the faces within the community and campus.

As we work with EDI initiatives in our campuses, there are simple ideas that help guide our work in diversifying library collections. This process of diverse library collections should not be a difficult process but rather something that opens up new ideas and creativities to further our mission in libraries and mirrors our community and our campus. These ideas are:

1. Scanning our library collections.
2. Awareness of personal biases.

3. Creating simple diversity statements.
4. Awareness of ethnic affiliates and acquiring their book award winners.
5. Intentional acquisition of materials by authors of color.
6. Reinforcing library collections with library programming/services.
7. Engaging with public libraries and other partners.

In this chapter, I am proposing that we look into the concept of belonging, from Maslow to Strayhorn, to diversify our library collections. Sense of belonging or belongingness is a significant factor that human beings, our patrons, strive for. Maslow and others, in fact, defined belonging as a basic human need for motivation, a behavior that impacts the way to interact and connect with others. In libraries, I want us to think of library collections as "living beings" with which our students, our patrons, interact and connect to satisfy the basic need for belongingness.

REFERENCES

American Library Association. (n.d.a). Library bill of rights. Retrieved from http://www.ala.org/advocacy/intfreedom/librarybill.

American Library Association. (n.d.b). ODLOS glossary of terms. Retrieved from http://www.ala.org/aboutala/odlos-glossary-terms.

American Library Association. (n.d.c). Professional Ethics. Retrieved from http://www.ala.org/tools/ethics.

Baumeister, R., & Leary, M. (1995). The need to belong: Desire for interpersonal attachments as a fundamental human motivation. *Psychological Bulletin, 117*(3), 497–529.

Bodaghi, N., & Zainab, A. (2013). My carrel, my second home: Inclusion and the sense of belonging among visually impaired students in an academic library. *Malaysian Journal of Library & Information Science, 18*(1), 39–54.

Freeman, T., Anderman, L., & Jensen, J. (2007). Sense of belonging in college freshmen at the classroom and campus levels. *The Journal of Experimental Education, 75*(3), 203–220.

Gant, A., Amsberry, D., Su, C., Munip, L., & Borrelli, S. (2019). International students and a sense of belonging: A case study at Penn State University Libraries. In Y. Luckert & L. I. Carpenter (Eds.), *The globalized library: American academic libraries and international students, collections, and practices* (pp. 99–118). Chicago, IL: Association of College and Research Libraries.

Hachey, V. K., & McCallen, L. S. (2018). Perceptions of campus climate and sense of belonging among non-immigrant, first-generation, and second-generation students. In K. M. Soria (Ed.) *Evaluating campus climate at US research universities: Opportunities for diversity and inclusion* (pp. 209–231). Cham: Palgrave Macmillan.

Hurtado, S., & Carter, D. (1997). Effects of college transition and perceptions of the campus racial climate on Latino students' sense of belonging. *Sociology of Education, 70*(4), 324–345.

Krogstad, J. M., & Fry, R. (2014). More hispanics, blacks enrolling in college, but lag in bachelor's degrees. Retrieved from http://www.pewresearch.org/fact-tank/2014/04/24/more-hispanics-blacks-enrolling-in-college-but-lag-in-bachelors-degrees/

Maslow, A. (1943). A theory of human motivation. *Psychological Review, 50*(4), 370–396.

Passel, J. S., Cohn, D., & Lopez, M. H. (2011). Hispanics account for more than half of nation's growth in past decade. Retrieved from http://www.pewhispanic.org/2011/03/24/hispanics-account-for-more-than-half-of-nations-growth-in-past-decade/

Pew Research Center (2012). The Rise of Asian Americans. Retrieved from https://www.pewsocial-trends.org/2012/06/19/the-rise-of-asian-americans/

Strayhorn, T. L. (2019). *College students sense of belonging: A key to educational success for all students.* New York, NY: Routledge.

We Need Diverse Books (n.d.). About WNDB. Retrieved from https://diversebooks.org/about-wndb/. Accessed on December 6, 2019.

CHAPTER 5

BE OUR GUESTS: CREATING UNIQUE AND INCLUSIVE LIBRARY EXPERIENCES

Sophia Sotilleo

ABSTRACT

The enhancement of technology and online access for libraries continues to be encouraging and convenient for all libraries and their patrons. However, there is so much that can be missed if we limit access to just online. Academic libraries offer key learning experiences and information that have become vital to its patrons, which can be missed if we are not being intentional about how we engage and interact with our patrons. Information literacy skill is identified as a key lifelong learning skill. This finding makes encouraging patrons to visit the library more important and yet challenging. This chapter will share some ideas and ways a small academic library increased their patron visits and usage of all resources by inviting patrons to "be our guests." Creating various ways to invite patrons in to learn and have an enjoyable experience sets the tone for how the library will and can be used for the rest of the patron's life. The quote by Charles William Eliot states that "The library is the heart of the university." Just like the heart sustains life, the library sustains the need for lifelong learning. Librarians have the opportunity to be intentional about how we encourage and create access to information that will keep our patron's moving toward academic success and the information literacy skills needed to become lifelong learners.

Keywords: Access; librarian; library; patron; information; literacy; learning

Hope and a Future: Perspectives on the Impact that Librarians and Libraries Have on our World
Advances in Librarianship, Volume 48, 43–50
Copyright © 2021 by Emerald Publishing Limited
All rights of reproduction in any form reserved
ISSN: 0065-2830/doi:10.1108/S0065-283020210000048005

INTRODUCTION

The quote by Charles William Eliot (2019) "The library is the heart of the university," is what I use often because it speaks to exactly how I view the Langston Hughes Memorial Library on the Lincoln University Campus. In the article "Human Heart: Anatomy, Function & Facts" the author shares in detail that the heart is an important organ designated to pump blood throughout the body via the circulatory system. It supplies oxygen and nutrients, removes carbon dioxide and other wastes from the body. The article reminds us that,

If the heart is unable to supply blood to the organs and tissues, and do the job that it has been created to do the organs and tissues will die (Lewis, 2016).

This is an important organ for the life and sustainability of our bodies. To use the heart as an analogy for the library gives a strong sense of how important the library is and the individuals that work and support its functionality. Each library wherever located, no matter how big or small, serves as a vital organ to its patrons. As library professionals we need to ensure that we are aware and engaged with our patrons to ensure we are supplying all the oxygen (conversations), nutrients (supplies and services), and removing carbon dioxide and other wastes (lack of access, limited collection and service) to our patrons so we, the library, do not die.

EVALUATING YOUR LIBRARY NEEDS

Every library environment is different. The patrons are different, which then ensures that the programming and other activities about the library and how it operates will be different. Libraries can be a place furnished with great authentic and expensive furniture with book collections beyond what anyone could ever read. It can also be an environment that is very small with the bare minimum of a collection and just enough furniture and staff to get by with assisting the community. Some libraries are friendly and inviting, a place you look forward to visiting frequently and encourage others to visit. Or, the library can be a place where you go to accomplish the bare minimum of tasks.

In the past, libraries were meant to be quiet places with the basic supplies of desks, lamps, books, and a staff to assist with locating and lending books. Patrons were told to be quiet if any sound made would cause a slight disturbance. In a recent study students shared that while the group study area was popular with some students, it also drew criticism from others: there were "too many people," " it was suggested that don't use because of congestion," " they were told to avoid, it was too noisy"(Khoo, Rozaklis, Hall, & Kusunoki, 2016) Which confirms some patrons still prefer the historical quiet space.

In the past, librarians were stereotyped where individuality was not shown. Especially in literature or movies, librarians were betrayed as bookish and portrayed as low paid workers (Peresie & Alexander, 2005). At the time, most librarians were women and were portrayed with glasses wearing a bun hairstyle and waiting for the opportunity to hush anyone making the slightest bit of noise. In the minds of many, the library wasn't an inviting place, but it was the best place to study, read, and conduct research. The library environment has changed and continues to change. With the increase of technology in the world and the changing mindset regarding collaborative spaces for working together, our library quickly decided that if we wanted to stay relevant, change was needed. At this time, patrons were beginning to challenge the need for libraries. Especially since many people believe that you can do everything online.

In our library we saw that Customer Service as well as the type of services offered to patrons had to be evaluated. Knowing what your library environment is and who your patrons are is the start to understanding what needs to change to ensure that you are relevant and meeting the mission and vision for your library.

BE OUR GUESTS – SHIFTING THE MINDSET

Maintaining the same kind of library environment was allowing our library statistics for visits and usage at the Langston Hughes Memorial Library to continue to decline. We didn't have many patrons, our circulation numbers were low, and other than our special collections department, there wasn't much being vocalized about the library. For an academic library, we didn't have many bibliographic/information literacy sessions being requested and only a small number of professors used the library for their research or as part of an assignment for students. It was at this time that our academic library quickly saw the need to make changes and work on ways we could shift toward meeting the needs of our patrons and become more relevant on our campus. The largest change was already in motion, a full renovation of the library. Once the library was renovated and reopened, we quickly began working toward a plan to allow our patrons the opportunity to utilize the new and improved library and library services. To begin this process, we started with a survey distributed to students, faculty, staff, and community to hear their voice and thoughts on how we were doing and where we could improve. The feedback received helped us to begin working on things to help the library be more of an inviting and workable space. The library staff had thoughts on what we needed to do as well so we also surveyed the library team to hear their thoughts and ideas. As you might imagine, some responses were a bit hard to accept. Everyone always thinks their service is impeccable and may need changes but not much. However, after reviewing and accepting the results of the survey the library staff began the much-needed work. We wanted the library to be more than just a place to utilize the computer lab and Wi-Fi capabilities or a walk-thru just for the restroom or access to another building during challenging weather. We wanted the library to be the place where thinking, collaborating, studying, and creating were taking place.

CUSTOMER SERVICE, GREETINGS WITH A SMILE

There is nothing like a friendly smile and greeting when you enter any establishment or place of business. Many companies have become intentional about placing someone at the entrance of an establishment to greet and direct customers as they enter a building. A personalized greeting can help make you feel special and it allows the patron to enter the space with a personalized invitation. It allows patrons a chance to slow down and experience the space even if it's for a quick visit. When you enter into a space and immediately encounter a welcome, a greeting, and a smile specifically for you, you begin to be mindful of the space and enjoy the time that you are in the location. Our goal was to try to give patrons the time to slow down and connect to the space they were in. Phase 1 of the process began with greeting patrons as they entered the library and acknowledging their presence at our location. Phase 2 added some form of assistance and service, reminding patrons that there was no request we could not assist with. Even if it was directional, we tried to offer it with a library twist. At first, patrons were a bit surprised, especially our students. A large percentage of our student population are the first-generation college students and very rarely asks for help. We quickly began to see patrons responding to our greetings and requesting assistance. We began to see more students visiting the library instead of just passing through. Phase 3 is where we offered a thank you gesture by offering water to groups having lengthy meetings in the library as a thank you for using the library as a meeting location. During finals week we began offering free coffee, tea, and hot chocolate for students studying until closing at 2 a.m. We collaborated and partnered with student organizations for snacks to go with beverages. We even began offering basic office supplies for patrons as needed. Folders, paperclips, index cards, and any items we could supply within our budget to ensure we were supporting patrons with their academic needs. Patrons appreciated the gesture and thoughtfulness that went into offering out of the box and extraordinary services. The opportunity to perfect the art of customer service, taking our idea of assisting and supporting our patrons for academic success to the next level was challenging and yet rewarding. The "be our guest" approach for our library began to change the patron's mindset about the library. Patrons knew that whatever was needed while they were in the library we would do our best to make it available. This type of service was a success. The "be our guest" customer service approach benefited the library with positive statistics as well as developed our professional relationship with patrons.

ROAMING REFERENCE/PERSONAL RESEARCH ASSISTANCE

Technology has allowed patrons to believe that it is possible to use Google to find any and everything. You believe that all of the information retrieved will be understood, credible, and accessible. Library professionals know what skill sets and expertise we have; and the more we share and utilize our skills with patrons less time will be spent trying to convince others of our value. One skill set we have is the knowledge to know that "GOOGLE" is just the beginning of any research process. Patrons were taken by surprise to see librarians step out from the reference desk to communicate with patrons in the computer labs and the open study areas asking if they needed assistance and showing interest in the work that they were doing. This human connection was the key to building a professional and academic relationship with librarians personally and sharing what expertise and skills librarians had to offer. This process opened up communication on a different level for additional and expanded assistance with assignments and asking questions. Librarians would listen to what was being requested or what assistance was needed and then offer the next step up or offer additional information to assist with requests. This interaction also assisted librarians with liaison work that was happening in various academic departments. We were also able to share our technology skills by assisting with technology and software issues as well. Our goal was to do our best to assist with each request completely. Once we allowed ourselves to be available to hear research ideas; or take the time to offer a more personal approach to assist patrons we were able to showcase our expertise and talents and open up the additional opportunity to be available and relevant to patrons.

NEW SPACE/MAKERSPACE

The space that you are in matters. Having an experience and enjoying and reflecting on being in a space and place that allows you to maximize your time is important. Libraries around the world have acknowledged this trend and have updated and remodeled spaces in various ways to ensure and enhance the opportunity for increased utilization. New spaces focused on furniture and space that will help with collaboration and working in groups, as well as space for personal study for different types of study patterns. The changes in architectural structure for new library buildings feature environmental and friendly designs. Designs include solar panels, high-efficiency HVAC systems, gardens, and waterfalls. Features that speak to promising a library experience to ensure you will return and use the library often. The cafe feature is also an approved enhancement to libraries that patrons appreciate. As much as library professionals worked to minimize food and beverages in the library, we are now one of the many places, especially in academic libraries that have cafes and or snack machines as part of the library spaces. Having a covered beverage nearby as you study or read is just part of the experience of spending time in the library.

Having designated spaces for collaboration also known as makerspaces that include special furniture, or technology enhances the meeting of the minds experience. Something as simple as a moveable dry erases board or a computer monitor that allows everyone to see and share work as the ideas and contributions are being made can make a difference when collaborating on a project or an assignment. Media rooms and multiple meeting and gathering rooms, additional computer labs are all a part of creating spaces to meet the multifaceted needs of patrons and the changing times of how people work together. The enhancement and willingness of libraries to change spaces to meet the needs of patrons have allowed patrons to reinvigorate or rethink wanting to spend time at the library. This translates to increased visits, usage of library resources, reference questions, and circulation of books, which is exactly what you want to see once you have invested millions of dollars to enhance a space.

COLLABORATION/PARTNERSHIP/BUY IN (INTERNAL AND EXTERNAL)

I believe that collaboration and buy-in are needed to support what librarians do daily. Collaboration and partnership on every and any level is important. Working with others helps us to share our vision with a stronger voice. This allows us to focus more on what we do and its relevance to our patrons. In academia, the library is necessary on every level of the college experience, as part of the curriculum as well as co-curricular activities. This is where the topic of embedded librarianship becomes such an important topic and work, especially in small liberal arts colleges and universities. All library support is needed to strengthen and enhance the relevance of the library in the environment and space that they are located in. For example, when the world continues to tell you that no one is using books, data shares how book circulation is on the rise. There are ongoing discussions about the lack of specific books by underrepresented authors, showing the need for more books to be published on certain topics by certain scholars. Librarians are being asked to be a part of discussions and to support and assist with literacy challenges in various education areas, to ensure that literacy can be less of an issue in communities and among people of color. It is the collaboration and support from others that assist with such demands and challenges and it is also what librarians do daily to continue sharing and showing our community our importance and relevance in the world. The skills that librarians have and the resources that libraries continue to strengthen and develop empower us to create and support our community in ways that are still being developed. Most importantly, it allows us to strengthen our skill set and work with others on what is needed and then develop and work toward enhancing all that we offer and do for patrons. The phrase "Team work makes the dream work" is just one of my favorite things to say when working with a team. First, it reminds me that the work that librarians do is enhanced when we work together. It also allows librarians to build a network of individuals and colleagues to advance the work that we do in a positive direction. Great things that happen aren't always done alone there is always a team that works together to design and execute the finished product.

PROGRAMMING: WE CAN DO THAT IN THE LIBRARY!

Historically, we know that there were certain things you could not do in the library. Especially if it involved any loud noises. Treasure hunts and electronic gaming activities? Absolutely not! Themed parties? Not allowed. Much of what we see taking place in libraries today is different from what was done in the past, and it's exciting. Librarians are becoming the innovators behind the ideas that allow and welcome programs that have changed how we use our library space. Innovative programming brings new people and ideas into the library, allowing everyone to be our guest. Innovative programming allows us to say, "If you are interested in being our guest we are willing to let you in." It opens up conversations that make it clear that we will support our guests' ideas with our resources. It is an exciting time when librarians look forward to interacting, supporting and meeting the needs of our patrons, which includes sharing the space for various types of programming and meetings. I do understand that this can be a challenge. It can result in wear and tear on the building that could cause budget concerns. At times, the programming can make you feel more like an event planner than a scholar or professional in the field, however, if you see ways to include the resources in the library with the programming or if you're partnering with the group it becomes a win–win for everyone.

When we connect our innovative programs with collaboration to meet the needs of our patrons, it makes all the hard work that went into planning and executing the events worthwhile. For me, it was a book display and reading for a 300-level English Creative writing course that sparked the change in programming for our campus and the increase in student's interest in our library collections. The student's final project allowed us to promote and display each student book of all of their short stories and poems created for the semester. We then planned a book read for the class. We picked a location in the library where all the books could be displayed, a podium was made available so that each student could read their favorite piece and share thoughts on their writings. We invited their family, friends, university administration, and the community to the book opening program, which included a reception after all of the presentations. Our school newspaper marketed the event and interviewed students for a write up in the school newspaper. This has now become a traditional program for this course. Every student gets an opportunity to self-publish on campus and launches their work in the library for a special program. We accomplished the goal of helping the first-generation students recognize that their voices and ideas do matter. We helped students visualize how libraries can support and become partners for their work and ideas. This program energized us to be innovative with our programming for our library with everyone we meet. With a focus on being intentional and inclusive, we ensure that all our patrons will "be our guests."

CONCLUSION

As we continue to evolve and work toward our Library mission and vision in our various libraries, and as we take time to be intentional about the work that we do, and the service that we offer it will become easier to have the "be our guest" mindset with our patrons. It will grant us the opportunity to share how the work of librarians and libraries can support the mission and vision of others. Librarians assist and support increasing student success in academics, literacy, community engagement and more. Libraries speak to lifelong learning and assist with job opportunities, social work issues, and social justice. Librarians can open up endless possibilities and information into being a part of the field of librarianship. The list can continue to be developed as we continue to partner and work together. I look forward to continuing the work by including the "be our guest" concept in various ways within my library each day, to let the world know that libraries and librarians are and always will be essential.

REFERENCES

Eliot, C. W. (2019). Retrieved from https://www.goodreads.com/author/quotes/4398096.Charles_William_Eliot

Khoo, M. J., Rozaklis, L., Hall, C., & Kusunoki, D. (2016). "A really nice spot": Evaluating place, space, and technology in academic libraries. *College & Research Libraries*, *77*(1), 51–70. https://doi.org/10.5860/crl.77.1.51

Lewis, T. (2016). *Human Heart: Anatomy, Funtion & Facts*. Retrieved from https://www.livescience.com/34655-human-heart.html

Peresie, M., & Alexander, L. B. (2005). Librarian stereotypes in young adult literature. *Young Adult Library Services*, *4*(1), 24–31.

CHAPTER 6

DIVERSITY AND INCLUSION: BETTER SERVING INTERNATIONAL STUDENTS AT ACADEMIC LIBRARIES

Jia He

ABSTRACT

With the globalization of education and immigration, international students have become a large population group at universities in the United States. However, language issues, adjusting to a new educational system, and culture shock are still big challenges for most international students. As a former international student majoring in Library and Information Science, the author deeply understands the difficulties that these students go through to achieve academic success in the United States. Therefore, when the author began working as the Liaison Librarian for International Students at the University of South Alabama in 2014, her first goal was to develop a relationship with related departments on campus to provide library services for these students. This chapter will provide a glimpse of the library outreach program created especially for international students at the University of South Alabama. This chapter will also share the author's professional experiences reaching out to different groups of international students and creating long-term collaborative working relationships with related departments on campus. The goal is to enable universities to create a welcoming library environment and provide services to support the academic success of all students.

Keywords: International students; academic library; library outreach; library orientation; information literacy; diversity

Hope and a Future: Perspectives on the Impact that Librarians and Libraries Have on our World
Advances in Librarianship, Volume 48, 51–57
Copyright © 2021 by Emerald Publishing Limited
All rights of reproduction in any form reserved
ISSN: 0065-2830/doi:10.1108/S0065-283020210000048006

LITERATURE REVIEW

Researchers have focused a lot of attention on international students in the past two decades to reach out to them, figure out the difficulties these students may have, and discover effective library services to help them at academic libraries. For example, Knight, Hight, and Polfer (2010) found that in spite of the fact that international students have become an important part of the student population at universities in the United States, they are still an underserved group at academic libraries. Baron and Strout-Dapaz (2001) pointed out that three challenges that international students have at the library are "language/communication problems; adjusting to a new educational/library system; and general cultural adjustments" (p. 314). Amsberry (2010) revealed that because of English deficiency, international students:

> may face several hurdles not experienced by their American counterparts. Such differing expectations can lead to accusations of plagiarism, which can then bring about consequences ranging from lost points on an assignment to severe academic penalties. (p. 31)

Another concern is that international students do not often interact with librarians when they need help at the library (Knight et al., 2010). Even for international students who do prefer in-person communication more than electronic methods, asking a librarian for help is not their first choice. Instead, international students often choose to ask their friends first, "followed by teachers, librarians, and Wikipedia" (Knight et al., 2010, p. 591).

Because librarians were concerned with helping international students in effective ways, they began looking at strategies to develop sustainable outreach programs for them. For example, Love and Edwards (2009) suggested that libraries and librarians build up collaborations and partnerships with student service units such as international student centers, study abroad programs, multicultural student services, career services, and writing centers to provide outreach services and establish relationships with international students. Langer and Kubo (2015) created a sustainable and manageable library outreach program for international students, which included "a library orientation for international students; information literacy workshops; library tours; and training for international peer advisors" (p. 609). Li, McDowell, and Wang (2016) recommended that multimedia video productions such as vernacular language videos are used to reach out to international students because "videos present an ideal means for connecting with a broad range of students, including international students" (p. 325). For example, language issues and cultural barriers can be solved by reaching out to international students via vernacular language videos, which will stimulate students' interest in using the library (Li et al., 2016).

BACKGROUND

International students have become a sizable group of the student population on university campuses in the United States. According to the Open Doors Report of the US Institution of International Education (2017b), the number of international students in the United States was 582,984 in 2007. Ten years later, this number increased by 85% to 1,078,822 (Institution of International Education, 2017b). In the state of Alabama, the population of foreign students was 9,549, which ranked 29th in the nation in 2017 (Institution of International Education, 2017a).

The University of South Alabama is a public university located in Mobile, Alabama. In 2017, with 1,391 international students enrolled, the University of South Alabama had the third highest number of international students in the state of Alabama (Institution of International Education, 2017a).

Prior to 2015, University of South Alabama Libraries offered no coordinated outreach program to these students. To remedy this, the Liaison Librarian for International Students was hired in 2014, and she created a library program especially for incoming international students at the University of South Alabama. The design ideas for this program come from the Liaison Librarian's previous experiences as an international graduate student and one-year work experience as Diversity Service Intern at the University of Wisconsin Milwaukee Libraries. This library program is comprised of outreach for incoming international students, library orientation, library tours, and information literacy classes, which aims to help incoming international students use library resources and services effectively and support their academic success.

To promote this program, the Liaison Librarian for International Students, with the support of the University Libraries Administration, collaborated with the Office of International Education and Global USA (Office of International Student Recruitment) to apply this program to incoming international students. Started in the Fall 2015 semester, this program has continued and has become a sustainable effort to benefit international students at the University of South Alabama.

EFFECTIVE OUTREACH TO INTERNATIONAL STUDENTS

As Langer and Kubo (2015) suggested, "it quickly became apparent that the best opportunity to reach large numbers of students was the campus international student orientation" (p. 609). International student orientation at the University of South Alabama is a required two-day event for incoming students before they begin their study. After contacting the staff at the Office of International Education and Global USA, the Liaison Librarian is given 15 minutes to present and introduce the University Libraries resources and services to the new international students at the orientation. Despite the limited time, the presentation makes a good first impression about the University Libraries among new international students. This gets the students interested in the library services and helps them feel comfortable asking librarians for help when they need it. After the presentation, the Liaison Librarian sets up a display table to represent the University Libraries at the browsing session during the international student orientation. The Liaison Librarian distributes her business cards to the students, introduces the library resources and services, and has brief conversations about their individual library needs.

Besides student orientation, the Liaison Librarian also reaches out to international students at other events on campus. For example, the International Spring Festival is an annual university event held by the Council of International Student Organizations and the Office of International Student Services at the University of South Alabama. It aims to promote international culture, interest, and knowledge through the efforts of both foreign and American students, faculty, and staff members. As the advisor of the Chinese Students and Scholars Association (CSSA), the Liaison Librarian led CSSA officers to promote Chinese culture at the International Spring Festival. Meanwhile, she used this opportunity to reach out to the officers from different international student organizations and build the relationships between the library and various groups of international students.

In her personal time, the Liaison Librarian helps new Chinese students and visiting scholars with their banking, housing, and grocery shopping at the beginning of each semester. This gives her the chance to talk to Chinese students and scholars in person and understand their library and information needs. Common questions from these students and scholars include how to find books and articles from the library catalog, how to avoid plagiarism, and how to improve their information literacy skills.

LIBRARY TOUR AND LIBRARY ORIENTATION

Initially, the library tours and library orientation for international students were conducted separately. From 2015 to 2017, the international student library tours were scheduled after the orientation at the request of Global USA and the English Learning Center. During the library tours, the Liaison Librarian showed students the locations of the elevators, study rooms, printers, scanners, and restrooms on each floor. She additionally introduced the library collections and services on each floor, distributed her business card to students at the end of tours, and welcomed them to contact her with their library questions.

Considering that most incoming international students still have English proficiency issues in listening and speaking, the Liaison Librarian tried to find librarians, staff, or student assistants who were able to fluently speak another language to help with the library tour, as it is much easier to understand the tour in one's native language. For example, in Fall 2016, a student assistant who is a native Arabic speaker in the Cataloging Department conducted five library tours with the Liaison Librarian for about 60 incoming international students from the English Learning Center. All the feedbacks from the students were positive.

After three years' effort of reaching out, the Liaison Librarian built a reliable collaboration with the Office of International Education and Global USA. It enabled the Liaison Librarian to conduct the library orientation, which combined the library presentation and library tour together for incoming international students. This was held at the university library auditorium starting in 2018.

Compared to the previous library presentation at the international student orientation, the library orientation was more visible and informative. The library orientation included a 25-minute library introduction session and a 15-minute library tour session. For the 25-minute library introduction session, the Liaison Librarian showed students how to use the University Libraries webpage to access popular library resources and services, such as the library's catalog, databases, e-book collection, and interlibrary loan. She also introduced students to the definition of plagiarism and the serious consequences of academic misconduct. Furthermore, she showed students different ways to get help such as the Ask a Librarian service, research consultation, and the Writing Center. After the presentation, a 15-minute library tour followed, which gave the students a direct and visible perspective about the library resources and services they just learned from the presentation.

All library orientation feedback from students was positive. Most international students thought the library was a convenient, peaceful, and friendly place to study and hang out with friends. Some of them showed strong interest in visiting the Writing Center in the library or asking librarians to help with their research questions.

INFORMATION LITERACY CLASS

It was a wonderful experience for the Liaison Librarian to collaborate with other departments to serve international students. The successful creation of information literacy classes was one of the most positive outcomes of this collaboration.

The first library instruction for international students was conducted in November 2015 at the request of an English as a Second Language (ESL) instructor at the English Learning Center. In the workshop, the Liaison Librarian taught students how to use the library's search engine, OneSearch, to find and filter materials related to the topics in their assignments. She also taught the students how to do advanced searches using Google. The librarian showed students the harmful effects of plagiarism and introduced them to Purdue Online Writing Lab to show different citation formats such as APA and MLA. Additionally, she showed students the LibGuide she created especially for international students.

Twelve international students from the ESL program attended the class and all their feedback was positive. Most students thought the workshop helped them understand how to use OneSearch, Google Advanced Search, and how to avoid plagiarism. Staff in the English Language Center said they would be pleased to recommend this class to more international students in the future.

Besides this, the Liaison Librarian also conducted information literacy classes for Chinese students and scholars in their native language. In March 2016, the Liaison Librarian conducted the first information literacy class for Chinese students and visiting scholars at the university library. In this class, she introduced how to use OneSearch, how to evaluate information resources, how to avoid plagiarism, and how to use reference management software such as Mendeley and Zotero. Seven Chinese students and visiting scholars attended this class. All their feedback was good and shows they are eager to attend more classes to improve their knowledge and information literacy skills.

The Liaison Librarian also coordinates and participates in English 102 library instruction in order to get more experience on how to prepare for the class, how to arrange class time, and how to help students with their research questions. She often sees international students at some of her English 102 classes, and this gives her the chance to help the students in person or set up a research consultation after the class.

THOUGHTS AND RECOMMENDATIONS

After five years of experience in outreach to international students, the Liaison Librarian has the following thoughts and recommendations to share with academic libraries and librarians. First, misunderstandings exist, which block international students from effectively using library resources and services. For example, research conducted by He (2019) revealed that library services such as course reserve, writing center, interlibrary loan, and research consultation are rarely used by international students. Why? Because these services are not provided at the libraries in most international students' home countries. Some international students do not use them due to unfamiliarity, and many do not realize such resources and services are provided to them at the University Libraries (He, 2019). Therefore, a library orientation to introduce available library resources and services should be provided to all international students on campus.

Second, there is frequently an overestimation of international graduate students' knowledge of the research process. He's (2019) study pointed out that unlike domestic graduate students, international graduate students rarely took classes to develop their research skills in their home countries before coming to the United States. In addition, entry-level information literacy classes, such as English 102, are typically only provided to undergraduate students. This means international graduate students may not have the opportunity to take any information literacy classes (He, 2019). Because colleges and universities assume international graduate students have taken research training in their original countries, they reason that these students should have enough research skills for their studies. Instructors also mistakenly believe the international students' level of information literacy is the same as their American classmates, which is often not the case (He, 2019). Therefore, it is necessary for academic libraries and librarians to provide targeted information literacy classes specifically for international graduate students.

Third, online library orientation and online information literacy classes should be considered as additions to the outreach program. There are many ways in which this could help. Firstly, international students' English proficiency issues can be resolved by adding subtitles to the videos of online library orientation and online information literacy classes (He, 2019). Additionally, time would no longer be a limiting factor. These online classes can be taken any time students are available and can be watched as many times as the students want (He, 2019). Lastly, once these online library orientation and classes are recorded, the videos can be shared with all international students on campus. This solves scheduling problems by reaching out to all international students at once (He, 2019).

CONCLUSION

This article briefly introduces the library outreach programs for incoming international students at the University of South Alabama. Composed of outreach for incoming international students, library orientation, library tours, and information literacy classes, this program aims to help incoming international students use the library resources and services effectively for their academic success. Starting from 2015, with the support of the University Libraries Administration, Office of International Education, and Global USA, this program has continued and has become a sustainable effort to benefit international students at the University of South Alabama. The author feels that similar programs would be beneficial to international students at other academic libraries.

With the increasing appearance of international students in university libraries, academic librarians need to be prepared to deal with the challenges from different cultures and different expectations. However, it is also a great opportunity for libraries and librarians to understand international students and provide effective services to support their academic success and address their unique information needs. As an immigrant to the United States, the Liaison Librarian for International Students understood that the library was not just a place to study and check out books, but it was also a secure place to assist immigrants with their transitions to a new country and culture. Therefore, academic libraries and librarians undertake an important mission to create a user-friendly and compatible environment not only for the sake of diversity but also for the benefit and improvement of the whole population.

REFERENCES

Amsberry, D. (2010). Deconstructing plagiarism: International students and textual borrowing practices. *The Reference Librarian, 51*(1), 31–44. doi:10.1080/02763870903362183

Baron, S., & Strout-Dapaz, A. (2001). Communicating with and empowering international students with a library skills set. *Reference Services Review, 29*(4), 314–326. doi:10.1108/00907320110408447

He, J. (2019). A comparative study of resource and service needs of international students at an academic library. *The Southeastern Librarian, 67*(1), 3–14. Retrieved from http://www.selaonline.org/sela/publications/SEln/issues.html

Institution of International Education. (2017a). Data by state fact sheets [Data file]. Retrieved from https://www.iie.org/Research-and-Insights/Open-Doors/Fact-Sheets-and-Infographics/Data-by-State-Fact-Sheets

Institution of International Education. (2017b). Enrollment [Data file]. Retrieved from https://www.iie.org/Research-and-Insights/Open-Doors/Data/International-Students/Enrollment

Knight, L., Hight, M., & Polfer, L. (2010). Rethinking the library for the international student community. *Reference Services Review, 38*(4), 581–605. doi:10.1108/00907321011090746

Langer, C., & Kubo, H. (2015). From the ground up: Creating a sustainable library outreach program for international students. *Journal of Library Administration, 55*(8), 605–621. doi:10.1080/01930826.2015.1085232

Li, X., McDowell, K., & Wang, X. (2016). Building bridges: Outreach to international students via vernacular language videos. *Reference Services Review, 44*(3), 324–340. doi:10.1108/RSR-10-2015-0044

Love, E., & Edwards, M. (2009). Forging inroads between libraries and academic, multicultural and student services. *Reference Services Review, 37*(1), 20–29. doi:10.1108/00907320910934968

CHAPTER 7

LIBRARY PROGRAMS FOR ADULTS WITH DEVELOPMENTAL DISABILITIES

Kayla Kuni

ABSTRACT

Library programs for developmentally disabled adults are essential for community enrichment. When the author created a program for her local library in 2014, she was a little alarmed by how few programs existed. Over the past few years, the author has seen a greater interest in programming for adults with developmental disabilities, but librarians have questions about where to get started. There are programs currently that are already available for those who want to engage developmentally disabled adults; however, librarians may also opt to create a program from scratch. For librarians who have never worked with developmentally disabled adults, there is some training available although it may not be what librarians really desire or need. The best opportunity to create beneficial programs is to collaborate with community partners such as local day training centers and schools.

Keywords: Adult programming; outreach; partnerships; collaboration; training; growth

Libraries have done an amazing job reaching out, and providing services, to young children and teens that are developmentally disabled. Are libraries providing that same level of service for adults with disabilities? In 2014, the New Port

Hope and a Future: Perspectives on the Impact that Librarians and Libraries Have on our World
Advances in Librarianship, Volume 48, 59–65
Copyright © 2021 by Emerald Publishing Limited
All rights of reproduction in any form reserved
ISSN: 0065-2830/doi:10.1108/S0065-283020210000048007

Richey (FL) Public Library established a program for adults with developmental disabilities (Kuni & Holtslander, 2015). The community of New Port Richey had several schools, or day training centers, for adults with intellectual disabilities. The schools' vans would pass by the library every day, but they never stopped at the library. Upon further reflection on the adult programs offered at the library, the staff realized that perhaps the library's adult programming was not of interest to adults with developmental disabilities and their families. A few other public libraries specifically had programming for adults with developmental disabilities, although none of those libraries were local. Staff sent emails to the libraries that did offer programming for adults with developmental disabilities to inquire about how to get programming started; staff received one response. The one response that was received, however, was very encouraging and motivated the library staff to pursue designing a unique program in concert with local day training centers.

TERMINOLOGY

The term "disability" is used frequently without any kind of distinction in what kind of disability is being discussed. There are, of course, distinctions in how disabilities are classified. The American Association on Intellectual and Developmental Disabilities (2019) defines intellectual disability as:

> a disability characterized by significant limitations in both intellectual functioning and in adaptive behavior, which covers many everyday social and practical skills. This disability originates before the age of 18.

Intellectual disability should be differentiated with the term developmental disability. The National Institute of Health defines developmental disability as:

> […] a severe, long term disability that can affect cognitive ability, physical functioning, or both. These disabilities appear before age 22 and are likely to be life-long. The term "developmental disability" encompasses intellectual disability but also includes physical disabilities. Some developmental disabilities may be solely physical, such as blindness from birth. Others involve both physical and intellectual disabilities stemming from genetic or other causes, such as Down syndrome and fetal alcohol syndrome. (National Institute of Health, 2018)

According to research compiled by Kraus, Lauer, Coleman, and Houtenville (2018), in 2016 about 12.8% of the US population had a disability; this number was an increase from 11.9% reported in 2010 (p. 1). The Center for Disease Control (2018), estimates about 15% of children between ages 3 and 17 have a developmental disability which can range from cerebral palsy, ADHD, hearing loss, among others. Libraries must make sure there is continuity in programming for all patrons across the spectrum of abilities.

PROGRAMMING FOR ADULTS WITH DISABILITIES

Some library staff may have noticed that adults with disabilities are interested in utilizing children's services as well as children's programming. Libraries need to be mindful of having adults with developmental disabilities attending children's programs or referring their questions to the children's services department. Adults with disabilities are adults; programming for them needs to be tailored to the needs and interests of adult users. Ultimately, libraries need to be clear about their programming guidelines and follow any specified library policy when adults are expressing interest in attending programs designed for children. In the event that a day training facility for adults with disabilities inquires about bringing a class to the library, staff should make an effort to develop something specifically for the group. Staff needs to exercise good judgment. Ask questions of the day training center like: what is being studied in school right now? What are the objectives of the class that day? What sorts of activities are students inquiring about? Staff should create dynamic programming that will have an impact on the patrons without developing a program that may be perceived as for children. In my experience, programs that encourage collaboration and conversation with peers are the most ideal. Projects that require participants to follow multiple steps are also great for interaction. With my library's program, I found that students enjoyed projects that had multiple steps. Students had several opportunities to give up on the project, but those steps gave them moments to take a break, re-center, and realize that they had already completed several steps toward the completion of the project.

To be clear, programming for adults with developmental needs, should also involve the patrons in the planning of the program. Adults attending the classes should be asked what they want to learn about and what their interests are. When first beginning a program, these kinds of questions may be difficult and this is where partnerships with a local day training center are beneficial. However, if there are no local schools to consult, there is the option of putting out a community survey to see what kind of results come back. Making a survey available enables others in the community to know that a new program is coming and offer feedback and, potentially, support.

As noted by Grassi (2017):

> [...] There is no "one size fits all" program for patrons with disabilities. Instead, program planning is a spectrum. Some patrons may be interested in programs specifically targeting patrons with disabilities [...].

Establishing a program series that will appeal to adults with disabilities is not necessarily a difficult task, but it is one to consider when 12.8% of the population is cited as having a disability (Kraus et al., 2018, p. 2). Regardless of the size of population, library services need to be established for the enjoyment of all in the community. Library staff may consider programs already offered as effective programming for adult patrons with developmental disabilities. A monthly film series, or crafting for adults, may already be inclusive for all. However, there are some very interesting programs specifically designed for adults with developmental disabilities. The Next Chapter Book Club is a national program that began in 2002 at The Ohio State University (Next Chapter Book Club, n.d.). The Next Chapter Book Club is a great option for those that want to get something started in a timely manner. There is also the option to create one's own program from scratch. For librarians that go this route, it is recommended that research is conducted and that experts are consulted. In the instance that staff has no background working with adults with disabilities, and has limited access to experts, it is highly recommended that partnerships with local day training facilities are established.

TRAINING AND PARTNERSHIPS

Working with those who are living with developmental disabilities may require training. Colorado State University, through the Rutgers Cooperative Extension, offers an online training program for people that are interested in working with people that are developmentally disabled (Developmental Disabilities Training Series, n.d.). The Washington State Department of Social and Health Services offers in person Developmental Disability Specialty Training; however, this in person training is targeted at employees that would be working in living situations (Washington State Department of Social and Health Services, n.d.). The lack of training specifically for librarians and staff working with adults with developmental disabilities should not dissuade a library from establishing a program. In many cases, it is better to look at local organizations to see if there is some kind of training that can be tailored to the specific needs of the library. Grassi (2017) mentions in person training opportunities "offered by local disability awareness groups." With a lack of training, library employees may find it valuable to consider partnering with a local day training school that works with adults with developmental disabilities. Partnering with local groups is also beneficial so that library programs are not a duplication of services, but are instead programs that are needed and desired. One great example is the partnership between Kansas City's De Soto Library and

> [...] the school district's Access House, an adult cooperative community education and support service program designed to help disabled students (ages 18–21) function effectively and independently in their community. (Nord, 2015)

Librarian Janine Myers opted to host a film discussion at De Soto Library with the Access House group so that they could "[...] share ideas and get experience participating in a typical adult discussion [...]" (Nord, 2015). Myers began a partnership with a community organization already helping the people that Myers wanted to work with. Myers did not have to create something new, but instead just had to expand on something (film discussion groups) that many libraries have already done before.

LIBRARY ORGANIZATIONAL SUPPORT

In various library organizations, there are opportunities to learn more about working with adults with developmental disabilities. The Association of Specialized, Government and Cooperative Library Agencies has the Library Service to

Individuals with Physical, Learning, Social, Cognitive and Health Disabilities Forum. The mission of this forum is:

> [...] to inform library staff about the information, communication, technology and format needs of people with these types of disabilities and how to meet them through programs, guidelines, and the Internet. We will act as a forum for discussion, action and advocacy. (Association of Specialized, Government and Cooperative Library Agencies, n.d.)

The International Federation of Library Association (IFLA) also has a Library Services to People with Special Needs Section. The IFLA section focuses on a much broader group of people as it included those who are in hospitals as well as those who are experiencing homelessness (IFLA, 2018). Given the information that is available for library staff to reference, there will likely be some great future programming ideas; however, the program itself must have support from the library management team.

PERSONAL REFLECTION

When I first began working in libraries, the idea of reaching out to various community groups and organizations was not something that I thought I would be doing. I thought my job would entail me staying in the library and watching over the youth department. However, my Library Director, Susan Dillinger, encouraged me to assist Associate Director, Ann Scott, with outreach activities. Once I started working in outreach, I found that I enjoyed it and was actually good at it. When I think back to how programs get started, it first requires having a leadership team in place that encourages growth within the team. One quick way to engage the team is to hear ideas and (here is the important part) act on them. If staff is producing programming ideas, and nothing happens with those ideas after they are discussed, the team will stop producing ideas.

I worked in an environment that was supportive of finding ways to make things happen. The library had a budget for adult programming, but the program that I had in mind was not on the radar when the budget was initially developed and approved. I mentioned to several community members my idea for an art program for adults with disabilities and was overwhelmed with the response I received. Several community members donated a variety of craft supplies. Just a few of the donations were enough to last me well into the next fiscal year. Money is important for programming, but do not let money be the thing that impedes service. Look for supplies that are not currently being used and upcycle them. One art class utilized old magazines that had been on the "free" cart for almost a year.

Programming does not always have to involve projects or art. I also taught computer classes for adults with developmental disabilities. Classes had a capacity of seven students. Smaller numbers for this kind of program were ideal since there was a lot of interaction with each student. Generally, this group stayed the same so that we could build upon skills established in the previous month. Each month, I had the students pick the topic of study for the following month. If I was able do this program all over again, I would have made it weekly or twice a month. I found that students did not retain a lot of information over the course of a month. In each class session there were struggles with navigating the mouse and typing; however, I saw improvement in confidence in searching for information that students were interested in. For example, the month we looked over online job resources, most of the students were highly engaged in the class and were enjoying the content. I attributed a great deal of the program's overall success to the fact that the students were able to choose their monthly topics and they were excited to learn how to use the computer. If a program is not working, or has grown stale, change it. I went from offering a monthly art class to offering a monthly art class as well as a monthly computer class. Since there was demand for both, I felt that both needed to be offered. My ability to offer both programs hinged on a few things like support from my management team, meeting room availability, and availability of technology. Without a demonstrated need, and prior programming success, additional program development may have been a challenge.

Success of programming is not always easy to determine. Numbers may be used as a factor in determining how successful a program is, but this should not always be the case. Programming for adults with disabilities requires several skills, among them patience. A library may not provide the best service for a program designed for adults with developmental disabilities when only one staff member is running the program and the class size is too large. I always kept my class sizes to no more than 12 adults so that my students knew that they had my attention. When there were more students than I could reasonably handle, I ran into issues with students not feeling recognized or feeling left out. If a student was hitting a roadblock, they were likely to give up on the project.

CONCLUSION

Working with adults with developmental disabilities is beneficial to all. The program attendees benefit from the library program and the staff benefits from providing a need to the community. According to Trinity Lescallett (2017):

> One of the benefits of working with individuals from the Opportunity Center is that it has made us better librarians. Our staff has a greater awareness about people with disabilities – and their abilities.

Library staff must also be aware that they should not exclusively focus on programming. Grassi (2017) states that "[t]here's more to serving patrons with disabilities than just program development." Grassi (2017) goes on to discuss books by mail programs, as well accommodation request forms to further benefit patrons with disabilities. Nord (2015) provides a series of best practices that were compiled by Myers from De Soto Library. Myers includes information like planning programs a year out, being mindful in selection of materials, and the necessity of paraprofessionals presence during the program (Nord, 2015). If libraries train their staff well, and make good use of resources already available, programming will not be intimidating. Librarians do not need to start from scratch in developing meaningful programs for adults with developmental disabilities. In providing programming for adults with developmental disabilities, we are shifting from simply awareness to social justice.

REFERENCES

American Association on Intellectual and Developmental Disabilities. (2019). Definition of intellectual disability. Retrieved from http://aaidd.org/intellectual-disability/definition

Association of Specialized, Government and Cooperative Library Agencies. (n.d.). PluSCH. Retrieved from http://www.ala.org/asgcla/asclaourassoc/asclasections/lssps/plusch

Center for Disease Control. (2018, April 17). Facts about developmental diseases. Retrieved from https://www.cdc.gov/ncbddd/developmentaldisabilities/facts.html

Developmental Disabilities Training Series. (n.d.). Retrieved from https://www.online.colostate.edu/badges/developmental-disabilities/

Grassi, R. (2017, January 17). Libraries for all: Expanding services to people with disabilities. Retrieved from https://www.ila.org/publications/ila-reporter/article/55/libraries-for-all-expanding-services-to-people-with-disabilities

International Federation of Library Associations (IFLA). (2018, April 20). Library services to people with special needs section. Retrieved from https://www.ifla.org/lsn

Kraus, L., Lauer, E., Coleman, R., & Houtenville, A. (2018). *2017 disability statistics annual report*. Durham, NH: University of New Hampshire. Retrieved from https://disabilitycompendium.org/sites/default/files/user-uploads/2017_AnnualReport_2017_FINAL.pdf

Kuni, K., & Holtslander, L. (2015, September 15). You belong@ your library: Programming for adults with intellectual disabilities [Webinar]. Retrieved from http://www.programminglibrarian.org/learn/you-belong-your-library-programming-adults-intellectual-disabilities

Lescallett, T. (2017, September 13). Serving adults with disabilities at your library. Retrieved from https://ideas.demco.com/blog/serving-adults-disabilities-library/

National Institute of Health. (2018, June 30). Intellectual and developmental disabilities. Retrieved from https://report.nih.gov/nihfactsheets/ViewFactSheet.aspx?csid=100

Next Chapter Book Club. (n.d.). About us. Retrieved from https://www.nextchapterbookclub.org/about-us#history

Nord, L. L. (2015, January 5). Reaching out: Library serices to the developmentally disabled. Retrieved from http://publiclibrariesonline.org/2015/01/reaching-out/

Washington State Department of Social and Health Services. (n.d.). DDA specialty training calendar. Retrieved from https://www.dshs.wa.gov/dda/dda-specialty-training

CHAPTER 8

FROM CULTURAL TRADITIONS TO DIVERSE SUPERHEROES: STRATEGIES FOR BUILDING INCLUSIVE YOUTH COLLECTIONS

Jewel Davis

ABSTRACT

Creating inclusive youth collections that authentically reflect and empower our ever-growing diverse youth population is a discussion at the forefront of library youth services, K-12 classrooms, and youth advocacy and literacy organizations. This chapter highlights core strategies used to build inclusive library and classroom collections. These strategies include methods for finding, promoting, and evaluating diverse youth literature. The appendix provides a list of resources that support the core strategies and includes references for further reading and advocacy.

Keywords: Collection development; diversity in youth literature; inclusive youth literature collections; evaluation strategies; cultural authenticity; inclusive collections

Creating inclusive youth collections that authentically reflect and empower our ever-growing diverse youth population is a discussion at the forefront of library youth services, K-12 classrooms, and youth advocacy and literacy organizations.

Hope and a Future: Perspectives on the Impact that Librarians and Libraries Have on our World
Advances in Librarianship, Volume 48, 67–77
ISSN: 0065-2830/doi:10.1108/S0065-283020210000048008

This conversation is not new: for well over a century, youth advocates have called for more authentic and diverse representation in literature. Librarians serving youth hold an impactful position within the conversation, for they are one of the few gatekeepers that directly affect the selection of materials available for youth to read in schools and public libraries.

Librarians have a responsibility to intentionally select and evaluate diverse materials and actively advocate for more authentic representation. As an academic librarian working in a preK-12 curriculum materials center, I work with pre-service teachers, school library students, and practicing teachers and librarians on developing strategies for creating inclusive library and classroom literature collections. This work is a driving factor in my passion for librarianship. Authentic youth literature has the power to promote positive identity development, motivate struggling readers seeking representations of themselves, develop empathy and knowledge about underrepresented groups, and counter the persistent damaging narratives found throughout media.

This chapter will highlight the core strategies I teach in professional development workshops and education classes on building inclusive library and classroom collections. These strategies include methods for finding, promoting, and evaluating diverse youth literature.

STRATEGIES FOR FINDING AUTHENTIC YOUTH LITERATURE

Use Collection Resources Beyond Trade Reviews

Popular trade review journals (School Library Journal, HornBook, Voice of Youth Advocates, Kirkus, etc.) are vital resources in youth collection development, and they provide a wealth of information to librarians searching for materials to include in their collections. However, when focusing on the identification of diverse elements and authenticity in youth literature, it is important to use collection resources beyond trade reviews. Many of our most popular review journals have been critiqued for a variety of problems around the identification and analysis of diverse youth literature. Some of these issues include not explicitly identifying characters of color and native youth in genres outside of realistic and historical fiction, starring titles that have later been identified as having inauthentic representation, utilizing microaggressions and insensitive language to describe diverse elements in reviews, and not including reviews for titles from smaller publishers and presses where many people of color, indigenous peoples, and marginalized individuals publish. Relying on policies and practices that center trade review journals as primary review sources for finding inclusive and authentic materials may result in missing titles that have diverse elements and missing reviews that critically analyze diverse titles.

As youth advocates, we have the power to change issues surrounding trade reviews. Many advocates have recognized and called out problematic language in reviews and supported reviewer diversity and training initiatives. This has resulted in some trade journals being more explicit in identifying diverse elements (Kirkus) and providing cultural competency training and diversity resources for reviewers (SLJ and VOYA). Even with these new initiatives and changes, it is important to seek out nontrade reviews that critically analyze the authenticity of diverse elements in youth literature.

Purchase Award Titles from the American Library Association (ALA) Ethnic Affiliate Partners and Multicultural and International Divisions

Many librarians purchase our profession's most celebrated award winners, such as the Caldecott, Newbery, and Printz. Librarians should also purchase award winners from our ALA Ethnic Affiliate partners and multicultural and international divisions because these awards celebrate and recognize the underrepresented in our collections in the publishing industry and in our society. Many of the committees are made up of people from within the minority group or culture and provide a level of scrutiny and analysis in authenticity that is beneficial to librarians purchasing and promoting more authentic titles.

Purchase from Small and Independent Presses

Seeking out small and independent presses that focus on supporting authors and illustrators from underrepresented groups will help librarians not only find diverse titles trade review journals do not include, but also enrich their collections with materials outside of mainstream publishing and trends. These titles frequently provide stories and experiences of groups sometimes overlooked by mainstream publishers. All of the award winners from the 2018 American Indian Library Association, for example, were from small presses. To provide a more comprehensive inclusive selection of materials, librarians should seek titles outside of mainstream publishers, for they still publish an overrepresentation of materials featuring white, heterosexual, cisgender, able-bodied, neurotypical characters.

Utilize Curated Lists from Organizations Devoted to Promoting Authenticity in Youth Literature

It is easy to find diverse book list suggestions online, but it is important to question who created each list and if they applied anti-bias evaluation and analysis criteria to the titles. Many online diverse book lists have been found to highlight classic and contemporary titles that feature diverse characters in damaging and stereotypical ways. Beyond simply gathering diverse titles, librarians should ensure the authenticity of these books' representations. Using curated lists from organizations like We Need Diverse Books and Social Justice Books provides an additional level of analysis that helps ensure the titles librarians purchase are supported in their representation.

Search for Advocates Promoting Diverse Titles in Nontraditional Spaces

Many youth advocates promoting diversity and authenticity in youth literature can be found on book blogs and Twitter. Social media sites provide spaces for groups to build community as they discuss and critique materials in ways that traditional trade and scholarly publishing platforms do not. The conversations being held over social media are valuable, intellectual, and timely, and they are directly impacting the ways in which authors, publishers, and advocates are creating, analyzing, and purchasing materials. Use social media to find conversations around diverse books. Even for librarians who are not active producers of content, creating an account to follow advocates will help them to stay abreast of materials that are being celebrated and materials that are being critiqued.

TIPS FOR SELECTION AND PROMOTION IN READER'S ADVISORY, DISPLAYS, STORYTIMES, BOOKTALKS, READ ALOUDS, AND TEXT SETS

Reconsider the Diverse Materials That Have Been Promoted without Applying Adequate Evaluating Criteria

As the critical conversations and work around authenticity continue, some titles librarians have previously recommended or used may be discussed as having inauthentic representation. Take note of the conversation and find authentic material that can take their place. What was beloved to us or used in the past may no longer be what we should recommend to our youth. If librarians can't comfortably recommend the material to a member of the represented group, they should reconsider recommending it to anyone at all.

Promote Diverse Materials Beyond Holidays, Histories, and Heritage Months

There is a tendency to focus mainly on historical movements, holidays, festivals, and foods when promoting different cultural groups. It is important to highlight and celebrate the history and traditions of various cultures, but selecting a range of materials that also incorporate contemporary genres and current experiences of the group help show the wholeness of the culture and the breadth of materials available. Promoting materials that show diverse cultures in adventurous, fantastical, or futuristic settings provides representation outside of the delegated history and informational books we frequently display these cultures in. Promoting materials that highlight the rich complexity and intersectionality of diverse groups creates more humanized and less stereotypical narratives. These materials should not only be highlighted during heritage months, but also incorporated in text selections throughout the year.

Select Materials That Work to Decenter Normative Perspectives

The large representation of materials available that highlight white, heterosexual, cisgender, able-bodied, or neurotypical characters makes it easy to primarily select and promote those narratives. It is important to intentionally and consistently select and display materials that work to decenter normative perspectives by highlighting the voices and experiences of marginalized and underrepresented groups. While fewer in number than the overwhelming majority of normative texts, these decentering narratives are important and help counter the persistent and sometimes damaging portrayal of what is considered normative in our society. Seeking out voices and stories from the margins in both fiction and nonfiction is imperative to building inclusive collections.

Seek Out Titles with Casual and Background Diversity

Casual diversity can be defined as a book featuring a diverse character in a common everyday situation or adventure. While the story features a diverse character, the story is not about that character's diverse identity, but rather about the normal and casual everyday experiences we all have as humans. Background diversity provides diverse representation in the background illustrations and settings of texts. If people are present in the background, they should reflect the diverse makeup of people in our society. Promoting titles with casual and background diversity helps normalize the everyday actions and presence of underrepresented groups.

Promote Diverse Materials to All Groups, Not Just the Groups the Materials Represent

Get to know the diverse materials in your collection and promote them in the same way you promote other materials. Readers need materials that represent not only their own experiences but also the experiences of others who are different from them. Do not discount a material's potential popularity or the transformative learning experience that can happen when a reader is given a book that highlights difference or shows them someone different in a universal or relatable manner.

STRATEGIES FOR EVALUATING AND DISCUSSING MATERIALS

Seek Out Ownvoice Reviewers

When librarians consider a book with diversity present, they should search for how people within the diverse group perceive the book. It is imperative that we listen to, acknowledge, and take to heart the opinions of reviewers from underrepresented groups. Even if the book is a beloved classic, from a bestselling author, or one that you think will fly off the shelves, we need to acknowledge the critiques so we are informed about how materials are viewed outside our own experiences.

Listen to Conversations Surrounding Controversial Titles

As more advocates become involved in analyzing literature for authenticity, these conversations become louder and more impactful. Following the dialogue and publications around controversial titles can begin to teach us the critical evaluation strategies we should employ when reviewing titles and highlighting issues from groups we may not have previously considered. Many of the members of the See What We See coalition post frequently on social media about titles they are evaluating.

Utilize and Apply Anti-bias Guidelines and Toolkits

There are many anti-bias guidelines and toolkits available for the various types of media and materials librarians will be selecting for youth. Many of the resources provide questions and strategies in order to look for stereotypes, tokenism, and invisibility, to check relationships between dominant cultures and minority groups, and to consider cultural misappropriation. A few questions to use when evaluating materials are:

- Who is telling the story?
  - What is their background?
  - What qualifies them to tell this story?
- How are they telling the story?
  - Are there stereotypes or tropes present in the art or text?
  - Are there groups left out of the narrative who should be there?
  - Are the portrayals of cultures accurate?
  - How are the relationships between people portrayed?
  - Who has power in the relationship?
  - Who is delegated to a supporting or replaceable role?
  - Are elements from a culture copied without authentic context?

Consider Using Inauthentic Texts to Engage in Critical Discussion

Inauthentic materials can provide you with the opportunity to engage in critical discussion about the problematics of the text. These texts can be used to help students and teachers identify and critique inaccurate representations. Consider developing critical inquiry-based book discussions for students and teachers. In these discussions, you can provide questions based on cultural theories, lenses, and perspectives that work to challenge misrepresentation. Providing space for critical discussion of inauthentic texts is a powerful strategy that can help participants recognize and interrogate the social messages conveyed in literature. Critical discussion pushes beyond inclusive displays and collections into a space that empowers readers and provides them with their own tools for critical anti-bias evaluation, action, and creation.

CONCLUSION

Promoting representative, inclusive, and empowering literature for youth is a major part of why I persist in librarianship. This critical work matters and has the potential to positively impact young readers. Decentering traditional collection development practices and utilizing alternative resources to find and evaluate diverse youth literature are important steps in creating inclusive collections and developing cultural competence in critical anti-bias evaluation. Revising collection development policies to reflect these practices provides a vital step in creating more inclusive institutional collection development practices. Incorporating the selection and promotion strategies into daily interactions with patrons helps bring underrepresented narratives from the margins into the mainstream. As these strategies are incorporated and become more commonplace, critical discussions can occur and help produce change in terms of representation in media. As you select, evaluate, and promote materials, consider these final questions:

- What stories, voices, and experiences are well represented in your collection?
- Whose stories are not represented or have only limited, stereotypical representations?
- Whose stories do you promote and make visible in your programs, displays, and reader's advisory?
- What stories would your patrons tell about people who are different from them if they could only create from the materials you have in your collection?

APPENDIX: RESOURCES

Below is a list of resources that support the core strategies and offer items for further reading and advocacy.

Selection and Evaluation Resources

Diversity Book Blogs and Websites

- Africa Access Review. http://africaaccessreview.org/
- American Indians in Children's Literature. https://americanindiansinchildrensliterature.blogspot.com/
- The Brown Bookshelf. https://thebrownbookshelf.com/
- CrazyQuiltEdi. https://campbele.wordpress.com/
- Cynthia Leitich Smith's Diversity lists. http://cynthialeitichsmith.com/lit-resources/read/diversity/
- De Colores: The Raza Experience in Books for Children. http://decoloresreviews.blogspot.com/
- Disabilities in Kidlit. http://disabilityinkidlit.com/
- Gay YA. http://www.gayya.org/
- I'm Here. I'm Queer. What the Hell Do I Read. http://www.leewind.org/
- I'm Your Neighbor. http://www.imyourneighborbooks.org/
- Latinxs in Kid Lit. https://latinosinkidlit.com/
- The Pirate Tree: Social Justice and Children's Literature. http://www.thepiratetree.com/
- Rich in Color. http://richincolor.com/
- Talk Story's Asian Pacific American Book List. http://talkstorytogether.org/asian-pacific-american-book-list/

Awards from ALA Ethnic Affiliate Partners and Multicultural and International Divisions

- American Indian Library Association Youth Literature Awards. https://ailanet.org/activities/american-indian-youth-literature-award/
- Asian Pacific American Librarians Association Awards for Literature. http://www.apalaweb.org/awards/literature-awards/
- Association of Jewish Libraries' Sydney Taylor Book Award. https://jewishlibraries.org/Sydney_Taylor_Book_Award
- Ethnic and Multicultural Information Exchange Roundtable's Coretta Scott King Awards. http://www.ala.org/rt/emiert/coretta-scott-king-book-awards-all-recipients-1970-present
- Gay, Lesbian, Bisexual, and Transgender Round Table's Stonewall Book Awards. http://www.ala.org/rt/glbtrt/award/stonewall/honored
- International Board on Books for Young People's Outstanding Books For Young People with Disabilities. http://www.usbby.org/obypd.html

- National Association to Promote Library and Information Services to Latinos and Spanish Speakers and Association for Library Service to Children's Pura Belpre Award. http://www.ala.org/alsc/awardsgrants/bookmedia/belpremedal/belprepast
- Schneider Family Book Award. http://www.ala.org/awardsgrants/awards/1/all_years
- United States Board on Books for Young People's Outstanding International Books. http://www.usbby.org/oibl.html

Small Press and Independent Publisher Lists

- CCBC's small presses owned and operated by POC and Natives. https://ccbc.education.wisc.edu/books/pclist.asp
- Monica Edinger's independent presses list. https://medinger.wordpress.com/independent-presses/

Organizations Devoted to Promoting Authenticity in Youth Literature

- Children's Book Council, CBC Diversity. http://www.cbcdiversity.com/
- Social Justice Books. https://socialjusticebooks.org/
- We Need Diverse Books. http://weneeddiversebooks.org/
- Worlds of Words. http://wowlit.org

Advocates in Social Media

- #WeNeedDiverseBooks
- #ownvoices
- Reading While White. http://readingwhilewhite.blogspot.com/
- See What We See coalition. https://socialjusticebooks.org/about/see-what-we-see/
- See what we see Coalition Members

  - @crazyquilts. https://twitter.com/crazyquilts
  - @readingspark. https://twitter.com/readingspark
  - @zettaelliott. https://twitter.com/zettaelliott
  - @booktoss. https://twitter.com/booktoss
  - @MarilisaJimenez. https://twitter.com/MarilisaJimenez
  - @teachingchange. https://twitter.com/teachingchange
  - @sojustbooks. https://twitter.com/sojustbooks
  - @debreese. https://twitter.com/debreese
  - @mariposachula8. https://twitter.com/mariposachula8
  - @Ebonyteach. https://twitter.com/EbonyTeach

Critical Evaluation

- Social Justice Books' Guide for Selecting Anti-Bias Children's Books. https:// socialjusticebooks.org/guide-for-selecting-anti-bias-childrens-books/
- Teaching Tolerance's Reading Diversity Lite: A Tool for Selecting Diverse Texts. https://www.tolerance.org/magazine/publications/reading-diversity
- #Act4teens: The Inclusive Library: More than a diverse collection – Part 1 (http://yalsa.ala.org/blog/2015/03/07/act4teens-the-inclusive-library-more-than-a-diverse-collection-part-1/) and Part 2 (http://yalsa.ala.org/blog/2015/03/21/act4teens-the-inclusive-library-more-than-a-diverse-collection-part-2/)
- Karen Jensen's Diversity Book Audit resources. http://www.teenlibrariantoolbox.com/2017/11/doing-a-diversity-audit-understanding-your-local-community/
- Tricia Ebarvia's how inclusive is your literacy classroom really? https://blog.heinemann.com/heinemann-fellow-tricia-ebavaria-inclusive-literacy-classroom-really
- Kidmap's DIG checklist. https://www.joinkidmap.org/digchecklist/
- See What We See Coalition Critical Reviews. https://socialjusticebooks.org/reviews-by-rating/

Further Reading and Advocacy

Background and Statistics on Diversity in Youth Literature

- Chimamanda Ngozi Adichie's Danger of a Single Story Ted Talk. http://www.ted.com/talks/chimamanda_adichie_the_danger_of_a_single_story
- Christopher Myers' The Apartheid of Children's Literature. http://www.nytimes.com/2014/03/16/opinion/sunday/the-apartheid-of-childrens-literature.html
- Cooperative Children's Book Center's Annual Statistics on Multicultural Literature in Publishing. http://ccbc.education.wisc.edu/books/pcstats.asp
- Diversity in YA's LGBT Statistics. http://www.diversityinya.com/tag/statistics/
- Edith Campbell's 50 Years of Diversity in Young Adult Literature. https://docs.google.com/document/d/1PVuxIihW4_3gAab-CHT5W0RXH-61F0HeD6ouy1yMFOac/edit
- Kathleen Horning's Milestones for Diversity in Children's Literature and Library Services. https://journals.ala.org/index.php/cal/article/view/5768
- Lee and Low's Diversity Baseline Survey & Diversity Gap in Children's Book Publishing 2018. http://blog.leeandlow.com/2018/05/10/the-diversity-gap-in-childrens-book-publishing-2018/
- Walter Dean Myers' Where are the People of Color in in Children's Books? http://www.nytimes.com/2014/03/16/opinion/sunday/where-are-the-people-of-color-in-childrens-books.html

Book Reviewer Training Resources

- SLJ Reviewer Resources. https://contributors.slj.com/
- VOYA Resources. http://voyamagazine.com/reviewers/

Intellectual Freedom Resources

- Selection & Reconsideration Policy Toolkit for Public, School, & Academic Libraries. http://www.ala.org/tools/challengesupport/selectionpolicytoolkit
  - Review Resources. http://www.ala.org/tools/challengesupport/selectionpolicytoolkit/reviewresources
- Defending Intellectual Freedom LGBTQ+ Materials in School Libraries. https://standards.aasl.org/project/lgbtq/

SECTION 3

CREATING COMMUNITY

CHAPTER 9

LIBRARIES AND THE CREATION OF INFORMATION ACCESS DESERTS

Conrad Pegues

ABSTRACT

Information is the most valuable commodity in the world, but everyone does not have equal access to information. Lack of equal digital access is an information access desert. Libraries should be public spaces to meet the digital needs of the community. Due to socio-political neglect, urban and rural public libraries cannot always meet patron needs. There is a pattern where urban libraries are either closed or cannot meet the demands for digital access until gentrification when upper class people move in and demand new libraries with sufficient digital access. Rural libraries suffer a similar fate with insufficient digital access to meet the economic and educational needs of their communities. Information access deserts identify a crucial issue for equal access to all regardless of economic status.

Keywords: Class; digital access; disenfranchised; gentrification; information; information access desert

INFORMATION ACCESS DESERTS

Digital mediums are a fact of modern life and the need for access is crucial to navigate modern society. It is common to use various electronic tools like smart phones, desktop and laptop computers, and tablets, but there is still an issue with

Hope and a Future: Perspectives on the Impact that Librarians and Libraries Have on our World
Advances in Librarianship, Volume 48, 81–89
Copyright © 2021 by Emerald Publishing Limited
All rights of reproduction in any form reserved
ISSN: 0065-2830/doi:10.1108/S0065-283020210000048009

access to the information that would be processed by these electronic tools. It can be taken for granted that everybody knows how to use digital tools but it's not always the case. An additional issue is the fact that everyone does not own comparable digital tools to effectively navigate today's digital world. To not be able to adequately navigate the digital world creates an information deficit that impacts the quality of life.

Information is any form of collected knowledge that orders and makes sense of the world. Digital information is any form of collected knowledge obtained by electronic means (i.e., phones, computers, or tablets). Access is the means by which an individual can get to the particular knowledge he or she needs.

Lack of digital information access can be caused by economics, location, education, and training. Because of this, libraries have become the frontline for people who might have limited or no access to digital information in their homes or communities.

For example, while working at the Hadley Park branch library in the Nashville Public Library system I noticed some of my patrons used free government cell phones with limited minutes as opposed to smart phones. They sometimes needed to download large caches of data like housing and job applications or information from government and medical sites. In addition, such phones may range from 250 to 1,000 minutes per month. If those minutes are depleted some patrons' budgets do not allow for the purchase of additional minutes. If that same person came to the library to use the computers they might not know the difference between a computer application, a mouse or a web page and how to navigate web pages for information necessary for their livelihood.

Hadley Park branch library opened in 1952 as the segregated branch for black people living in North Nashville and currently sits in an area slowly undergoing gentrification. North Nashville is an economically impoverished area where crime is an issue and during my tenure as branch manager Hadley Park was often referred to as a "problem branch" along with Looby Branch in North Nashville and Pruitt Branch in South Nashville of the Nashville Public Library system. Many Hadley Park patrons would openly complain that Hadley Park did not have comparable offerings of study rooms, larger selections of books, and a certain ambiance of libraries in affluent areas of the Nashville Public Library system like the Green Hills branch. Respecting patron concerns, I became conscious of the quality of library spaces and the particular issues an economically impoverished area might have when it came to information access.

Information access is not to be wholly confused with the so-called digital divide. Digital divide would be the stock term to describe the lack of skills to access computers in the library. Merriam Webster defines digital divide as "the economic, educational, and social inequalities between those who have computers and online access and those who do not" (Digital Divide, 2018). Information access is a digital divide issue, but more specifically I will explore the issue of lack of access for people due to demographic and socio-economic shifts caused by gentrification as well as historical factors pre-existent to the digital divide in race and class. I dub such spaces information access deserts.

Information access deserts are created by economic duress and political neglect whether intentional or the default of pre-existent factors such as race, class or geographic location. News, jobs, housing, education, research needs, medical information, government access, politics, social media, and general social contacts call for digital access. The digital divide is a matter of the skills to use computer technology, but information access deserts are the lack of access to the conduit of information in equipment and the physical space of libraries. Such factors as gentrification, race, and class are the symptoms of information access deserts, but they are problems created by human beings who do not see information access as a social justice issue of equal access for all.

GENTRIFICATION AND INFORMATION ACCESS

Gentrification is a common phenomenon in large cities in the United States as well as around the world with the influx of middle and upper class people to neighborhoods that for years were traditionally all black, of an ethnic mix and/or working lower class. Or they were neighborhoods that were once predominantly white but due to white flight from "black encroachment" or loss of industry, whites moved to other, usually suburban areas. This often took place during the 1960s and early 1970s of the twentieth century. It was about this time sociologists began to study the reasons and effects of such metropolitan migrations on neighborhoods and the people who inhabited them.

Gentrification is a term coined by sociologist Ruth Glass in 1964 with her observation of poor communities being taken over by other classes in London, England. At present, the term is applied to blacks, Latinos and/or the working poor who are pushed out of established neighborhoods due to rising property costs, reduced availability of affordable housing and a general feeling of not being wanted in an area that no longer reflects their common history and experience. This can take place house by house or block by block and will not be referred to as gentrification in some political circles, but "urban renewal" which James Baldwin in 1963, a year before Ruth Glass coined the termed gentrification, dubbed "negro removal" (Baldwin, 1963). Gentrification has a more salient impact on groups that have a history of historical disenfranchisement.

> Gentrification commonly occurs in urban areas where prior disinvestment in the urban infrastructure creates opportunities for profitable redevelopment, where the needs and concerns of business and policy elites are met at the expense of urban residents affected by work instability, unemployment, and stigmatization. (Slater, 2010, p. 572)

During the shifting of the demographics across race and class whole areas go through a process of losing necessities for people to maintain a viable lifestyle including grocery and drug stores, restaurants, housing, social structures, and viable libraries. It is not only an issue of affordability but a general lack of the basics of life and an established historical sense of community and family that is erased.

German activist Andrej Holm identified three stages of gentrification to impact poor and disenfranchised neighborhoods. Schuldt and Blumer (2014, p. 1) frame Holm's stages of gentrification as it concerns libraries and in particular

the neighborhood of Flon in Lausanne, Switzerland. In the first stage of gentrification, crime is prevalent, there are neglected and abandoned properties and
rent is low. In the second stage, people move in for the cheaper rents including
artsy types who have little social capital, but alter the cultural landscape. In the
third stage, people with economic capital move in, buildings are either renovated
or torn down for new construction, rent goes up, and the socio-economic culture
shifts with chain grocery stores and specialty shops that the original occupants of
the area cannot afford.

Blumer and Schuldt look at the impact of gentrification on libraries as
impacted by the demands of class. In the first or second stage of gentrification, libraries are either overwhelmed with computer technology needs or closed
altogether to "become part in processes of the repulsion of socially vulnerable
groups" (Schuldt & Blumer, 2014, p. 1). Schuldt and Blumer (2014, p. 9) note that
in the third stage of gentrification, libraries are built or renovated to meet the
needs of the new class of patrons in the area who have more money and political
power than the previous occupants.

Although Blumer and Schuldt describe the pattern of gentrification and libraries in Lausanne, Switzerland, the pattern remains the same across cultures and
countries. In Lausanne, Switzerland, the classes of people immediately impacted
were the poor and over time with the slow process of gentrification drug users and
a criminal element squatted in Flon before it was taken over by urban renewal
projects. Libraries follow the trend of poor or no services for the original occupants of the area to better services as the gentrification process completes its cycle
to the benefit of people with money and political power (Schuldt & Blumer, 2014,
p. 9).

GENTRIFICATION, RACE, AND INFORMATION ACCESS DESERTS

Blumer and Schuldt look at class and gentrification as it impacts library availability and access, but the same pattern of gentrification can impact historically
disenfranchised groups in America. Information access deserts are created by
economically challenged areas that impact black and brown communities.

For example, many black people in the Frayser area of Memphis, Tennessee,
would fall into a class of patrons facing information access deserts with larger
library needs and limited library facilities in an economically depressed area.
According to Memphis Library Director Keenon McCloy (Dries, 2013) in the
Memphis Library System a small 6,400 square foot branch like Frayser has a high
demand for computers:

> No matter what time of day you go, it is packed with people who are either looking for jobs,
> waiting for computers, checking out books. It's an extremely busy branch.

Frayser is approximately 84% African American and 13% White in an area once
dominated by working class whites until the exodus of business and industry in
the 1980s. Frayser is now one of the poorest areas in Shelby County after the

flight of major industries like International Harvester and Firestone (Community LIFT, n.d., p. 9). There are nineteen branches in the Memphis Public Library system with Frayser being one of the smallest to serve 45,000 residents in the area and is in need of larger facilities to better serve the Frayser area (Turner, 2016). In the stages of gentrification, Frayser is at stage one in an economically depressed area with high crime and specifically impacts the information access needs of that community.

Overcrowded libraries become part of the information access desert land-scape in economically depressed areas. Black people native to Frayser or who have moved there with poor whites for affordable housing are information access deprived with limited computer skills, computers, and internet access. All of these factors impact job prospects, social stability, and higher crime rates. Information access and its quality or lack thereof are interminably connected to economics and history and how historically disenfranchised groups are framed within their communities.

Another intersection of gentrification, race, and libraries is happening in Chicago, Illinois. News of the Obama presidential library to be constructed on the South Side of Chicago, an area dominated by black people disproportionately facing economic distress, crime, and blight alarmed residents as "a covert means to continue the displacement of Chicago's Black residents" (Renegade, 2015). In an interview, community activist Natalie Moore initially questions the impact of gentrification and the South Side of Chicago:

> The University of Illinois at Chicago and Harvard University both conducted studies on Black South Side neighborhoods and concluded the neighborhoods didn't gentrify. Green doesn't trump Black. In Bronzeville, Black professionals moved in with a range of salaries, but the amenities, the retailers and some of the investment didn't come. Research is showing gentrification is overplayed in Black communities, and [gentrification's ability to thrive] has to do with perception. Because we're segregated, people in other parts of the city are like, "I'm not coming to the South Side." It's this blanket, big, Black, ghetto where there are shootouts on the corner every weekend. (Harvey, 2016)

Although Moore says "Green doesn't trump Black" it is a matter of time when "green" will trump poor black people and they will be wholly displaced by real estate developers, city planners, and the political machine to make the South Side a hot commodity to accommodate more affluent Chicagoans, many of whom will be wealthy whites. With the usual pattern of gentrification, comes depletion of basic resources, lack of policing, which feeds higher crime rates, food deserts, depression of real estate values to later become inflated real estate values and taxes, and higher prices for goods and services. Regardless of Moore question-ing gentrification's impact on the South Side, she is part of a coalition to create a community-based agreement between the South Side and the Obama Foundation including the library and community developers to protect the South Side from displacement (Moore, 2017). The South Side is at stage 2 of Holm's gentrification model in some areas and stage 3 in others.

The Obama presidential library will bear the latest technologies and informa-tion access for those living in the immediate area as well as those who can afford to travel to it. It can be stated a library is for everybody, but what happens in gentrification is that black people and other historically disenfranchised groups are pushed out through various legal means of stringent code enforcement, over-priced housing and land. Once gentrification is well under way in an area, librar-ies are firmly established to meet the needs of the new occupants of an area.

GENTRIFICATION, CLASS, AND INFORMATION ACCESS DESERTS

Information access deserts readily impact poor or working class people and their information access needs, but gentrification is not the only means through which information deserts are created. Sometimes economic disparities are preexistent due to geographical location and lack of political advocacy. Rural areas are just as much in need of information access as big cities because of the rise of technol-ogy in modern society.

There is a history of economic duress impacting libraries in rural areas. During the 1930s it was estimated 45,000,000 people lacked public library service and about 22,000,000 of those were people in the Southeastern United States (Wilson, 1937). The Great Depression of the early twentieth century (1929–1939) exacer-bated lack of library access for poor people across the United States. President Franklin D. Roosevelt attempted to counter the lack of library access in areas miles away from large cities lacking roads and the means to reach them with the Works Progress Administration (WPA). The WPA provided work for librarians to meet the information needs of the underserved or unserved. The WPA cre-ated "200 new libraries, more than 3400 new reading rooms, and 5800 traveling libraries" (Digital Public Library of America, n.d.). Regional libraries and mobile library services were created to meet the library needs of a wider geographical area unlike urban counterparts with a number of small branch libraries over a general area.

Presently, under economic duress, libraries are struggling with increased patron needs and less funding and access. What was once an issue of access to books in the early part of the twentieth century has become an issue of digital information access in the twenty-first century. The difference between the 1930s and the present is not just rural areas cut off by rivers and no roads, but large non-urban areas that are underserved due to insufficient funding and services or no library service at all.

> In a survey of rural librarians in Tennessee, respondents reported that their patrons' most criti-cal information need was broadband Internet access. The respondents also ranked access to recent hardware technology and software, technology training, and help with specific tasks like applying for jobs or government benefits as highly critical. By comparison, the respondents ranked traditional services such as book loaning as the least critical duty, significantly trailing the above mentioned and other technology services. Despite rural librarians viewing technol-ogy-based services as their most important function, however, rural libraries lack the resources to meet the same service quality as non-rural libraries. (Real, Bertot, & Jaeger, 2014)

For example, the rural library system of Scott County, Tennessee, has three small libraries, Huntsville Branch, Oneida Branch, and the Winfield Branch, for approximately 22,000 residents in an area considered by the state of Tennessee to be "economically depressed" (McGhee 2017, p. 1A). The Huntsville Branch alone has 10 public terminals. The need for internet access is exacerbated by increased unemployment issues and residents who don't have sufficient internet access to search for jobs because of economic factors. Scott County is faced "with an unemployment rate hovering above 18 percent and another 400 jobs lost in a span of months due to the loss of industry" (McGhee, 2017, p. 1A). Scott County's response is to attract internet carriers into the area for increased speeds and wider offering where on average there are three houses per mile. The problem is still one of costs per household and internet education three libraries cannot easily ame-liorate as well as the financial expense of computers in the household. Poverty and information access deserts counter the job search process in an age when many companies only post job listings online and require online applications as opposed to paper applications.

As essential as libraries are, both urban and rural, they should not be in the position of pandering for money to meet public demands that are no longer as simple as checking out books and movies. Libraries help uplift and sustain the quality of people's lives.

CONCLUSION

Information deserts are made by oversight and neglect on a social and political scale. Too often libraries are seen as expendable and low on the scale of impor-tance because of antiquated ideas of what libraries do and mean to the socio-economic stability of whole communities. Libraries are no longer outlets for the latest *New York Times* bestseller, movies or newspapers. They are outlets help-ing to maintain the vitality of neighborhoods and the people who need them for wider services just to survive. Arguments to close libraries because patrons check out DVDs and use computers more than they check out books is mislead-ing when the powers that be do not understand the modern uses of the library with information access.

Pew data showed a reduction in library use due to lack of advertising of broader services beyond the traditional offering of books and reduced funding to maintain the modern digital needs of libraries and their patrons (Crum, 2016; Meyer, 2016). Funding directly impacts advertising dollars to let patrons know what services are available to them in finding jobs, housing, digital access, and instruction. Even if advertising is in place, libraries must have sufficient equip-ment, technologies, and personnel to assist patrons in their needs and those needs must be met within local areas for access.

America is a capitalist society, but information should never be subject to the whims of the economic market especially as information is the number one com-modity worldwide (Amer & Noujami, 2019). Libraries are not a business and cannot be judged on the generation of capital like a business model. Libraries create social capital which must be protected and maintained for the welfare of the larger populace. Advocacy to put an end to information access deserts must include librarians, patrons and politicians to keep libraries viable and offer equal access to all no matter the stage of gentrification or geographical location in urban or rural areas.

As was mentioned earlier in this piece, the library branch I managed from 2013 to 2015 in the Nashville Public Library system Hadley Park in North Nashville is in an area of gentrification between stages 2 and 3 by Holm's model. As one resident of North Nashville has put it "50 percent of the neighborhood has flipped over or is on its way to flipping over" (Hale, 2018).

Librarians can help to counter the problems of information access deserts through advocacy that looks nothing like traditional librarian roles.

As recently as the Covid-19 pandemic libraries had to be included in the CARES ACT to provide financial assistance to burdened state infrastructures. No doubt some would not reopen after the pandemic due to the lack of funds or funds being transferred to other areas deemed "essential." Advocacy by American Library Association (ALA) provided guidance to the Department of Education on how those monies should be used for library digital efforts for quarantined citizens and vulnerable library staff (ALA, 2020).

Advocacy also can take place in the form of letter writing campaigns. For example, the District of Columbia proposed to eliminate libraries and librarians altogether from their educational programs. Opposition arose from many library organizations including the Black Caucus of the ALA and the American Association of School Librarians which voiced their concern to the DC school board (Save School Librarians, 2017). Because of vocal public advocacy, the DC school board only cut some librarian programs, but no librarians lost their job. It's a small victory but a victory just the same as the school board originally considered eliminating all librarian programs which would have created an information access desert in the schools themselves.

Librarians have to become politically savvy to stop the creation of information access deserts. Librarians have to learn not only advocacy, but political strategy and city planning, creating alliances with neighborhood organizations and political caucuses and go as far as running for political office to give libraries and librarians a voice in our political discourse.

Historically disenfranchised groups of race and class will suffer the most under information access deserts creating a misinformed and permanent educational underclass for generations. By its nature, a democratic society must allow information access to everyone or it is no longer a democratic society. Libraries are a means to make America true to its ideals of democracy and freedom of information.

REFERENCES

Amer, K., & Noujami, J. (2019). *The great hack*. Los Gatos, CA: Netflix.

American Library Association (ALA). (2020, April 4). To "Secretary of Education Betsy Devos." Retrieved from http://www.ala.org/advocacy/sites/ala.org.advocacy/files/content/libfunding/school/ALA%20Letter%20to%20Secretary%20DeVos%20pdf%20final.pdf

Baldwin, J. (1963, May 24). *An interview with James Baldwin* [Television Broadcast]. Boston, MA: Open Vault with WGBH Media Library & Archives. Retrieved from http://openvault.wgbh. org/catalog/V_C03ED1927DCF46B5A8C82275DF4239F9

Community LIFT. (n.d.). Frayser Data Book. Retrieved from http://www.communitylift.com/sites/ default/files/datafiles/Frayser%20Data%20Book.pdf

Crum, M. (2016, April 4). Library attendance is declining: Here's why. *The Huffington Post*. Retrieved from https://www.huffingtonpost.com/entry/library-attendance-study_us_570fdeade4b0561c9f04264d

Digital Divide. (2018). Merriam Webster.com. Retrieved from https://www.merriam-webster.com/ dictionary/digital%20divide

Digital Public Library of America. (n.d.). A history of U.S. public libraries. Retrieved from https:// dp.la/exhibitions/exhibits/show/history-us-public-libraries/libraries-on-the-move/wpa-library-programs

Dries, B. (2013, May 17). Study details library usage, sparks call for more funding. *Memphis Daily News*. Retrieved from https://www.memphisdailynews.com/news/2013/may/17/past-due/

Hale, S. (2018, June 7). History repeats itself in North Nashville. *Nashville Scene*. Retrieved from https://www.nashvillescene.com/news/cover-story/article/21007855/history-repeats-itself-in-north-nashville

Harvey, S. A. (2016, March 23). The south side offers a new take on an old problem: Segregation. *Colorlines*. Retrieved from https://www.colorlines.com/articles/south-side-offers-new-take-old-problem-segregation

McGhee, J. (2017, January 9). Where the internet grows. *The Tennessean*, pp. 1A, 9A.

Meyer, R. (2016, April 14). Fewer Americans are visiting local libraries—And technology isn't to blame. *The Atlantic*. Retrieved from https://www.theatlantic.com/technology/archive/2016/04/ americans-like-their-libraries-but-they-use-them-less-and-less-pew/477336/

Moore, N. Y. (2017, September 18). A wary south side eyes Obama's return. Retrieved from https:// www.citylab.com/design/2017/09/a-wary-south-side-considers-obamas-return/540168/

Real, B., Bertot, J. C., & Jaeger, P. T. (2014, March). Rural public libraries and digital inclusion: Issues and challenges. *Information Technology and Libraries*, *33*(1), 6–24. Retrieved from http://link. galegroup.com/apps/doc/A371174114/AONE?u=tel_k_wsideel&sid=AONE&xid=0e1a8dee

Renegade, G. T. (2015, May 17). Is the Obama Library a weapon of gentrification? Retrieved from http://atlantablackstar.com/2015/05/17/obama-library-weapon-gentrification/

Save School Librarians. (2017). Retrieved from https://www.saveschoollibrarians.org/d_c_increases_ education_budget

Schuldt, K., & Blumer, E. (2014). Urban revitalization, gentrification, and the public library: The case of Lausanne, Switzerland. LIBREAS. Library Ideas. Retrieved from http://libreas.eu/ ausgabe26/03blumer/

Slater, T. (2010). Gentrification of the city. In G. Bridge & S. Watson (Eds.), *The New Blackwell companion to the city* (pp. 571–585). Oxford: Blackwell.

Turner, L. (2016). Frayser library branch plays vital role in community. *High Ground*. Retrieved from https://www.highgroundnews.com/features/frayserlibrary.aspx

Wilson, L. (1937). Library service in rural areas. *Social Forces*, *15*(4), 525–530. doi:10.2307/2571424

CHAPTER 10

THE VISUAL AND PERFORMING ARTS IN LIBRARIES

Caley Cannon

ABSTRACT

This chapter examines the impact and influence of the visual and performing arts in sustaining thriving communities and highlights the essential role of libraries in providing access to arts and cultural programming and services. Creative and artistic intervention has become the imperative of our time. Creativity is required not only in design studios and workshops, but in all areas of work and life, both professional and personal. Places of artistic and cultural production are strongly correlated with strong local economies and sustainable communities. Libraries are public spaces that promote and maintain community, not only civic institutions. As such, the library plays a key role as incubator for the arts. Libraries advocate freedom: of ideas, communication, and information. Arts programming in libraries provides an avenue for people to communicate ideas and feelings through visual, auditory, or kinesthetic forms. But more than that, libraries are also about education, safe and welcoming spaces, community, and entertainment. Libraries support and promote the value of multiple perspectives and voices. Libraries can shape patronage of the arts and engage future generations by addressing social diversity and inciting inclusive participation in the arts. Many libraries are participating in the creation of new forms of understanding through arts programming, services, and resources. In an age where many of society's most important challenges are related to our relationship with information, it is vitally important to include visual and performing arts professionals in the intersection between artistic practice and critical engagement with information.

Hope and a Future: Perspectives on the Impact that Librarians and Libraries Have on our World
Advances in Librarianship, Volume 48, 91–99
Copyright © 2021 by Emerald Publishing Limited
All rights of reproduction in any form reserved
ISSN: 0065-2830/doi:10.1108/S0065-283020210000048010

Keywords: Visual art and libraries; performing art and libraries; creative communities; creative economy; community and libraries; art and critical thinking

INTRODUCTION

This chapter will examine the impact and influence of the visual and performing arts in sustaining thriving communities and highlight the essential role of libraries in providing access to arts and cultural programming and services.

Creativity is touted as important and vital to the health of communities, both now and in the future. Yet, the creative process is frequently misunderstood or bemoaned as a scarce resource. For many, creativity is a rare gift bestowed on exceptional people – the "artistic genius." However, according to Cronin and Loewenstein (2018), creativity is a learnable skill that means developing different ways of thinking and receptiveness to changing perspective. Creativity is an internal process (a journey), not the end result or a single moment. This ongoing effort to build new approaches takes time and willingness to face uncertainty, failure, and criticism. Managing emotions and maintaining motivation is part of the craft of creativity. Personality traits most associated with creativity include willingness to take risks, tolerance for ambiguity, openness to experience, and willingness to face uncertainty and turn it into excitement and hope (Cronin & Loewenstein, 2018, p. 193).

Creativity is possible in anything we do. The urge to create is evident throughout human history and intertwined with human progress and involves distinct habits of mind and patterns of behavior that must be cultivated by individuals and surrounding society (30,000 Years of Art, 2019). Creativity requires a supportive environment so how can we nurture the type of environment that fosters and supports creative effort?

HUMAN DEVELOPMENT AND THE ARTS

The influence of the environment on the developing human brain has been the subject of numerous research studies. Children need stimulating experiences and carefully designed environments that offer interesting and complex learning opportunities (Shore, 2015). Visual, auditory, tactile, and kinesthetic arts are stimulating and engaging and satisfy a child's insatiable quest for learning.

Listening to complex music and learning to interact with music as soon as possible (even before birth) can wire a child's neural circuitry in complex networks needed for spatial-temporal and language-analytic reasoning (Shore, 2015, p. 108). This type of reasoning is needed for math, performing music, chess, puzzles, visualizing different options of placement and organization, moving objects in space, and problem-solving, in other words, the ability to recognize patterns and relationships. It seems that listening to complex music builds complex neural networks, which improves hand–eye–ear–mind skill combination, auditory skills, language, and reading.

Music creates a foundation for more than cognitive development, however. Music develops a sense of community and social cohesion. The social and emotional effects of music extend the range of human communication beyond words and pictures. Music is often referred to as the universal language, spanning all cultures and throughout history (Gottlieb, 2019).

Music is a key part of what makes a place authentic and it plays a central role in the creation of identity and formation of real communities. Musical memories are some of the strongest and most easily evoked (Florida, 2014, p. 295). The benefits of music are not limited to listening or playing an instrument; singing is good for us as well. The act of singing together increases endorphins and improves self-confidence and general well-being. Singing has an aerobic component and increases circulation and oxygen in the blood, which has a positive impact on mood. Singing also requires breathing and breath awareness, which reduces anxiety.

Some of the benefits of music and singing are based on rhythm and studies have shown that rhythmic interactions (such as music and dance) connect people (Taylor & Murphy, 2014, p. 246). Dance involves expressing ideas through motion in space and time. Spatial brain development and vertical eye tracking are essential to learning to read and moving around (Shore, 2015, p. 82). Freedom of movement develops motor skills and a wide range of motions and prolongs life by encouraging physical activity and healthy habits.

Arts participation has significant benefits across many academic spectrums as well. When young people are engaged in creative arts from an early age, they outperform their peers in every category including academics and life skills (Taylor & Murphy, 2014). Children that regularly participate in arts programs have improved test scores, more positive perceptions of school, respect for others, better self-esteem, and overall better attitudes and behaviors (McCarthy, Ondaatje, Zakaras, & Brooks, 2004).

Dramatic play (such as theater) improves language and math performance and school engagement by encouraging verbalizing, storytelling, embellishment, and anticipation, all of which stimulates higher-level thinking and verbalizing skills (Shore, 2015, p. 84). Nearly every American believes the arts are part of a well-rounded K-12 education (91%). The vast majority of Americans (89%) say the arts should also be taught outside of the classroom in the community (Americans for the Arts, 2018).

The importance of the arts and creative expression cannot be overstated. The arts shape our understanding of who we are and what it means to be alive in the world. Engaging in creative activities elicits joy by enhancing awareness of the present moment and self-expression. The arts strengthen human expression and the ability to demonstrate empathy by responding to others' emotional expressions. The sense of vitality and meaning in the present moment brings down walls and builds trust (Taylor & Murphy, 2014, p. 18). To reach full potential, creativity requires cultural heterogeneity and early exposure to ideation diversity and conflict, and the cross-fertilization of ideas, beliefs, and meaning (Florida, 2014).

LIBRARIES AND ARTS – CHANGE AGENTS

Arts and cultural professionals are increasingly involving themselves in questions of community development: how do we want to live together? (Ziehl, Rabe, & Haupt, 2016). Places of artistic and cultural production play an important role in the sustainable community. The arts are a driving force in economic development. Artists are often those responsible for opening new spaces and paving the way for new culture beyond the established limits and standards (Ziehl et al., 2016, p. 13). Essentially, the arts and cultural engagement becomes a lifestyle for the community.

Socioeconomic theories, such as the Creative Class thesis popularized by Richard Florida, have advanced the view that creative industries are a key driving force for economic development. Creative and artistic intervention has become the imperative of our time. Creativity is required not only in design studios and workshops but in all areas of work and life, both professional and personal. Ziehl et al. (2016) argues that we should become the artisans of our own lives (p. 14). We can respond to the issues of our time with creativity and flexibility, looking for new solutions and areas of action.

For this to be effective, art and creativity must be valued as a culture that thrives in the long term and permanently bears fruit, not merely as a culture in the form of individual projects that need resources in certain places during limited funding periods or merely a commodity to be bought and sold (Ziehl et al., 2016, p. 17). A thriving arts scene is enrichment for the whole of society and enhances the sustainability and resilience of human communities. This requires a place for cultural exchange between different groups of society. Libraries are a natural fit for this role.

SPACES OF POSSIBILITY

Libraries are public spaces that promote and maintain community, not only civic institutions (Wiegand, 2015). The library plays a key role as incubator for the arts, an idea explored by Damon-Moore and Batykefer (2014). Libraries advance social, educational, and creative values, and play a key role in cultural diplomacy by promoting understanding. Fostering the exchange of knowledge and experience and encouraging creativity often require confidence building, skills training, human networks, civic participation, risk taking, and intercultural understanding (Lord & Blankenberg, 2015, p. 23). Libraries can support these goals and advocate for participation in culture activities as an effective means of creating an open civil society.

Libraries advocate freedom: of ideas, communication, and information. Arts programming in libraries provides an avenue for people to communicate ideas and feelings through visual, auditory, or kinesthetic forms. But more than that, libraries are also about education, safe and welcoming spaces, community, and entertainment. Libraries support and promote the value of multiple perspectives and voices (Garmer, 2014).

The creativity community model outlined by Taylor and Murphy (2014, p. 29) integrates creative process, social application, group dynamics and interactive, and intergenerational learning. Like libraries, creative communities are all about participation and inclusion. Everyone is invited. Interestingly, 7 in 10 Americans believe the arts unify their communities; and 2 in 5 Americans have changed an opinion or perception based on an arts experience (Americans for the Arts, 2018). The arts enable us to connect with our own humanity across generations and cultures and form collaborative partnerships in exciting new ways.

COMMUNITY-FOCUSED

Places of artistic and cultural production are strongly correlated with strong local economies and sustainable communities. In Gallup International (2010), researchers discovered that the most highly valued attributes in communities are social and cultural amenities, friendliness and openness, and esthetics (natural and physical beauty). The "quality of place" is tied to what is there, who is there, and what is going on (Florida, 2014, p. 281). Despite globalization and technology, location and community are still highly valued, as are experiences that develop full human potential and creative capabilities. Libraries exemplify the sharing economy and social commons that provide space for people as well as build a sense of identity and trust in order to cohere as a community. Libraries are not the only institutions that recognize the importance of provided uplifting spaces for everyone. Museums are studying libraries to learn from their experiences (Lord & Blankenberg, 2015, p. 17). Many museums offer storytimes for children and families to connect literacy with art in the galleries. Libraries can take a similar approach by incorporating the arts in programs and events in the library and forming collaborative partnerships with local arts and cultural organizations to connect visitors to both spaces.

Placemaking is a multifaceted approach to community building that recognizes that places and spaces embody an idea that brings a person's whole being into the lived experience (Parker, 2018, p. 55). Libraries can be beautiful, accessible, and meaningful spaces to meet, exchange ideas, and solve problems. Libraries are anchor institutions – proven sites of community sustainability, accumulated knowledge, engagement with the public, and sites of community participation (Lord & Blankenberg, 2015, p. 21).

Investment in developing full human potential and the creative capabilities of every person is needed for advanced nations to thrive and prosper. We are currently experiencing major social changes in the United States that increase the need for safety, security, and attachment/belonging. Widening gaps in wealth, income, and education reveal that America is becoming more divided and unequal: by income, employment, education, politics, culture, health, and happiness. We hear about group differences constantly in the news, television, radio, and social media. The potential to tap into the fear caused by these changes is great. We need to understand the changes and find ways to increase our sense of security to better reduce the distance between individuals and groups.

Our individual and collective well-being depends on our ability to understand others and help them understand us. Visual exhibits can use images and artifacts that teach us about other people. We can explore the lives of others through literature, theater, music, and dance. Library programs can encourage empathy, curiosity, tolerance, creativity, and critical thinking, thereby enlightening us about the lives and perspectives of others.

Developing social empathy in this way helps us to see the world as others see it and experience it, revealing the context of life situations. Empathy is fundamental to bridging diverse people and communities and leads to thriving, prosperous individuals and communities (Segal, 2018, p. 30). Empathy helps us navigate social situations and feel a sense of well-being. Enhanced empathy across groups creates communities that are cohesive, caring, and successful. Understanding the situations of others so we can better connect and minimize misunderstandings will help us overcoming tribal/group bias and serves as an antidote to the "otherness" divide that contributes to prejudice, discrimination, and oppression (Segal, 2018, p. 57).

Prosocial behavior, that is acting in a supportive and helpful way, is more likely when we can empathize with others. Overcoming barriers of fear and skepticism directly relates to the question: "How do we want to live together?" Soft power is the ability to influence behavior based on ideas, knowledge, values, and culture, not force or finance (hard power) (Lord & Blankenberg, 2015, p. 9). Community-focused institutions, such as libraries, play a role in building cultural infrastructure. Libraries are strong, socially minded networks that can employ soft power to accelerate cultural change and empower citizens to be more inclusive. How can libraries exercise more influence and be of greater value to their communities?

One way is by creating meaningful, memorable experiences with purpose. Being thoughtful and intentional about programs, services, and partnerships connects the library to the development of the community and its culture. One of the key roles of art is to induce uncertainty or wonderment about social and cultural phenomena. Art makes us think and reflect critically. Libraries can provide spaces purposefully designed for exchange and invite participation with visual and performing arts programming that makes interactions between people happen.

Consciously bringing people together for a reason shapes the way we think, feel, and make sense of the world (Zebracki & Palmer, 2018). Libraries provide an audience of every kind of person in the community, thereby celebrating collective and individual experiences. The basic principles of democracy include the freedom to assemble, exchange information, and inspire each other. Equality and the sense of belonging is also connected to Abraham Maslow's theory of the hierarchy of needs, which is often used to study human motivations and behaviors. The need for security, safety, understanding, and belonging provides an opportunity for creative dialogue that libraries are in a unique position to provide.

Libraries can shape patronage of the arts and engage future generations by addressing social diversity and inciting inclusive participation in the arts. Many libraries are participating in the creation of new forms of understanding through arts programming, services, and resources. In an age where many of society's most important challenges are related to our relationship with information, it is vitally important to include visual and performing arts professionals in the intersection between artistic practice and critical engagement with information. Many libraries have embraced this exciting opportunity!

ARTS + LIBRARIES IN ACTION

Madison Public Library in Wisconsin has an artist-focused program called The Bubbler that establishes the public library as a platform for creative and innovative art events, shows, and workshops with an emphasis on local creators. The program includes an artist residency, exhibitions, and learning opportunities for all ages. The Seattle Public Library works with artists in residence on creative projects both on and off site. Programming includes music and dance performances and art exhibitions in the library gallery. Similarly, the Artists on Site residency program is a partnership between Brooklyn Public Library and Brooklyn Arts Council, to bring diverse cultural heritage and contemporary art practices into branch libraries throughout their system.

The New York Public Library for the Performing Arts houses one of the world's most extensive combinations of circulating, reference, and rare archival collections in its field. A wide range of special programs, including exhibitions, seminars, and performances, are offered throughout the year. Los Angeles Public Library produces special-edition library cards designed by local artists. The library works with artists to create these limited-edition cards to celebrate the place (the library) that ignited their imagination. The library also includes multiple exhibition spaces that highlight local history. The acclaimed ALOUD literary series includes performances to draw a connection between diverse creative modes of expression. The Los Angeles County Libraries have partnered with the LA County Arts Commission and board of supervisors to offer a summer concert series in public sites around the county. The musical artists featured represent the diversity of the region and a broad range of genres.

Brand Library & Art Center, in Glendale, California, has been a cornerstone for the arts in Southern California since 1956. This unique public library is focused on visual arts and music and provides free services, collections, and programs for a diverse community, including subject specialist librarians, exhibitions, concerts, lectures, dance performances, films, and hands-on craft programs for all ages. Brand Gallery presents a professional gallery experience for the community. The curated exhibitions offer an array of art by established and emerging artists that reflect a variety of media, styles, and cultures and provide diverse viewing experiences. An annual juried show, sponsored by the Associates of Brand Library, draws entries from across the country from artists that choose paper as their primary material. The annual dance series began in 1974 and features site-specific dance designed for nontraditional performance spaces. The goal is to take advantage of the unique architecture and setting of Brand Library and incorporate dance into the exterior areas of the building and surrounding park. The annual chamber music series and outdoor summer concert series regularly draw standing room only crowds with a diverse and eclectic range of performers. Recently, the ReflectSpace gallery opened at the Central Library location in Glendale. This unique exhibition space is designed to explore and reflect on social justice issues around the world, such as genocide, immigration, violence in society, and slavery. Brand Library & Art Center and ReflectSpace are part of the city's Library, Arts & Culture department, which is working to integrate the visual and performing arts into all aspects of the community.

These are only a few examples of libraries that are doing outstanding work to create a central place for the visual and performing arts within the communities they serve. Libraries are models for effective programming, services, and resources that respond to community needs, act as change agents, and demonstrate cultural inclusion and competence, and value diversity.

CONCLUSION

Visual and performing arts programming in libraries benefits both patrons and artists/performers by providing a distinctive setting in which to experience the arts. Libraries provide an avenue to expand the boundaries of art and visual culture and offer opportunities for audiences to engage with this pluralistic, interdisciplinary environment. Exploring the relationship between dance, music, art, and literature promotes an understanding of the creative process of expression. In a setting that features a variety of creative outlets, these modes of human expression converge and present the opportunity to enhance creativity and awareness of self and others.

Multicultural communication is enhanced through creative expression as audiences can connect with a variety of cultures through dance, theater, music, and the visual arts. Libraries can provide the audience and artists/performers with a unique space and esthetic environment with which to explore creativity and artistic expression. Visual and performing arts programming is an opportunity for library staff to explore and establish partnerships with local community and arts organizations, schools, and creative professionals. Libraries can market their spaces as a unique venue in which to present nontraditional performances and exhibit in a community space.

Human development is enhanced through visual and performing arts education and cultural enrichment. The arts benefit all intelligences and learning styles, enhance academic achievement, develop creativity, require discipline and cooperation, offer different perspectives, provide options for self-expression, and deliver lifelong benefits, such as creating community and opening channels for greater communication and understanding. Free visual and performing arts programming, services, and resources in libraries make it possible for everyone to experience the benefits of the arts.

REFERENCES

30,000 Years of Art. (2019). *30,000 years of art: The story of human creativity across time and space.* New York, NY: Phaidon Press.

Americans for the Arts. (2018). *Americans speak out about the arts in 2018: An in-depth look at perceptions and attitudes about the arts in America.* Washington, DC: Americans for the Arts. Retrieved from https://www.americansforthearts.org/by-program/reports-and-data/research-studies-publications/public-opinion-poll

Cronin, M. A., & Loewenstein, J. (2018). *The craft of creativity.* Stanford, CA: Stanford University Press.

Damon-Moore, L., & Batykefer, E. (2014). *The artist's library: A field guide.* Minneapolis, MN: Coffee House Press.

Florida, R. (2014). *The rise of the creative class, revisited.* New York, NY: Basic Books.

Gallup International. (2010). *Soul of the community: Why people love where they live and why it matters: A national perspective.* Ann Arbor, MI: Inter-university Consortium for Political and Social Research (distributor). Retrieved from https://www.icpsr.umich.edu/icpsrweb/NADAC/studies/35532/publications

Garmer, A. (2014, October 14). Rising to the challenge: Re-envisioning public libraries. Retrieved from https://www.aspeninstitute.org/publications/rising-challenge-re-envisioning-public-libraries/

Gottlieb, J. (2019, November 21). New Harvard study says music is universal language. *The Harvard Gazette.* Retrieved from https://news.harvard.edu/gazette/story/2019/11/new-harvard-study-establishes-music-is-universal/

Lord, G. D., & Blankenberg, N. (2015). *Cities, museums and soft power.* Washington, DC: American Alliance of Museums.

McCarthy, K. F., Ondaatje, E. H., Zakaras, L., & Brooks, A. (2004). *Gifts of the muse: Reframing the debate about the benefits of the arts.* Santa Monica, CA: RAND Corporation. Retrieved from https://www.rand.org/pubs/monographs/MG218.html

Parker, P. (2018). *The art of gathering: How we meet and why it matters.* New York, NY: Riverhead Books.

Segal, E. A. (2018). *Social empathy: The art of understanding others.* New York, NY: Columbia University Press.

Shore, R. (2015). *Developing young minds: From conception to kindergarten.* London: Rowman & Littlefield.

Taylor, P., & Murphy, C. (2014). *Catch the fire: An art-full guide to unleashing the creative power of youth, adults and communities.* Gabriola Island: New Society Publishers.

Wiegand, W. A. (2015). *Part of our lives: A people's history of the American public library.* Oxford: Oxford University Press.

Zebracki, M., & Palmer, J. M. (Eds.). (2018). *Public art encounters: Art, space and identity.* New York, NY: Routledge.

Ziehl, M., Rabe, C., & Haupt, T. (Eds.). (2016). *City linkage: Art and culture fostering urban futures.* Berlin: Javis Verlag GmbH.

CHAPTER 11

AUTISM AND LIBRARIES: BUILDING COMMUNITIES AND CHANGING LIVES

Adriana White

ABSTRACT

Once synonymous with books, libraries now provide a growing number of community services. Simultaneously, autism rates have increased worldwide. Improved diagnostic criteria have given us a clearer view of autism's prevalence. Once thought to primarily affect nonverbal Caucasian males, we now know that autism crosses racial and gender lines.

As the diagnosis rate of autism grows, so too does the importance of libraries. Libraries are a vital community space – a place to safely interact with others and observe social norms. Libraries also house books and stories, which are critical to language and social development. As autistic adults age out of school-based programs, libraries provide access to technology and a sense of structure. Sensory-friendly libraries, with elements of Universal Design, are also benefiting the greater community – making libraries better spaces for all patrons.

As the number of autistic adults grows, so too does the number of autistic librarians. Generations of adults who grew up in the library are understandably being drawn to the profession. They are comfortable in the workplace and especially skilled for the job. Their input in the field should be encouraged.

Hope and a Future: Perspectives on the Impact that Librarians and Libraries Have on our World
Advances in Librarianship, Volume 48, 101–110
ISSN: 0065-2830/doi:10.1108/S0065-283020210000048011

This chapter aims to provide an overview of the importance of libraries to the autistic community and identifies libraries as a significant place that can help communities to better serve the autistic individuals in their area. Strategies and ideas for libraries will be shared. Libraries can also serve as a potential workplace for autistic adults, and more outreach should be undertaken to encourage autistic librarians.

Keywords: Asperger's; autism; libraries; library services; neurodiversity; training

INTRODUCTION

I Love Libraries.

As a novice librarian, I have only a few years of experience in the field of librarianship, but I happen to have several years of experience with being an autistic person in a library setting. Growing up, I saw libraries as magical places – enormous sanctuaries that held books, magazines, encyclopedias, movies, CDs, computers, and more. As a child in a military family, I moved often, but I always found a predictability and comfort in libraries. No matter where I found myself, I could navigate my way through a public library. I knew the rules and rituals of the library space. I could move through it with ease and automaticity. I felt like I belonged.

As an adult on the autism spectrum, I now see the magic of great library management and purposeful programming. Great libraries do not appear out of thin air – they are designed and facilitated by amazing library staff. Libraries have well-trained staff members who are deeply in tune with the needs of their communities, and who are willing to fervently advocate for their patrons' needs. When they discover that they have patrons on the autism spectrum, libraries are willing to go to great lengths to serve the needs of this special population. As a result, libraries are finding that autistic adults keep coming back– and some even return as librarians.

This chapter focuses on the significance of libraries to the autistic community, with an emphasis on how libraries can better serve their autistic patrons and support autistic librarians.

OUR WORLD TODAY

Libraries and Their Communities

More than just books and banks of computers, libraries are still places where individuals gather to explore, interact, and imagine. (Edwards, Rauseo, & Unger, 2011, p. 42)

Today's libraries are not just for checking out books. If you were to ask a group of patrons what they do at their library, you may find that you get an assortment of very different answers. Depending on who you ask, you may discover that patrons come to their library to:

- access the internet and technological devices;
- get advice on their resume or job search;
- vote in local, state, and national elections;
- file their taxes or fill out government forms; and
- learn a new language or skill, and more.

The idea of a library as a stagnant warehouse for books is based on out of date and incorrect ideas. Libraries are, and have always been, purpose-driven resource centers. An unorganized and uncurated collection of resources leaves patrons searching for the equivalent of a needle in a haystack. Librarians have been specially trained to analyze and organize enormous amounts of resources, and they deftly utilize these resources to guide patrons to the specific information they are seeking. Through their efforts, librarians work closely with a wide cross-section of individuals in their community: students, seniors, job-seekers, children, parents, teachers, and many others. As a result, libraries are uniquely positioned to identify key areas of need within a community. Today's libraries are also determined to fulfill those needs to the best of their ability.

The American Library Association (ALA) notes that libraries play a significant social role in their communities – providing public meeting spaces, staff expertise on a variety of topics, a safe space for kids and teens to gather after the school day ends, and access to technology for low-income patrons and job-seekers (ALA, 2019). Services like homework help, summer reading programs, and early literacy programs help improve educational outcomes in communities nationwide. Programs like storytimes, book clubs, and pop culture conventions are especially important for autistic patrons.

Autism, In Flux

First, a note on identity-first language: While "person-first" language – such as "person with autism" – has typically been the norm in academic circles, there has been a push in recent years toward "identity-first" language – such as "autistic person." For members of the autistic community, person-first language is seen as painting autism (and other disabilities) in a negative light. There is a shared experience to be found among individuals with similar brain structures, and identity-first language is a way to acknowledge and support that shared experience. This idea is also known more broadly as "neurodiversity." Author and autistic advocate John Elder Robison, writing for *Psychology Today*, had this to say about neurodiversity:

> To me, neurodiversity is the idea that neurological differences like autism and ADHD are the result of normal, natural variation in the human genome. This represents a new and

fundamentally different way of looking at conditions that were traditionally pathologized; it's a viewpoint that is not universally accepted though it is increasingly supported by science. That science suggests conditions like autism have a stable prevalence in human society as far back as we can measure. We are realizing that autism, ADHD, and other conditions emerge through a combination of genetic predisposition and environmental interaction; they are not the result of disease or injury. (Robison, 2013)

The idea that autism has been around for millennia is an important one. It reshapes a condition that has been viewed by some as an epidemic into something infinitely less frightening. Centuries-old stories of changelings, hermits, "deaf and dumb" individuals, absent-minded professors, and other odd misfits can now be viewed through a neurodivergent lens and reinterpreted as historical representations of what likely may have been autism. Since the term "autism" has only been in use since the early 1900s, there has not been a single term to define the wide range of the autistic experience over the course of human history.

Today, autism is estimated to affect 1 in 40 people (Wright, 2018). This number has sharply increased over the past six decades. As noted in a report on *Mental Disorders and Disabilities Among Low-Income Children*, initial studies on the prevalence of autism in the 1960s and 1970s led scientists to estimate that the condition only occurred in approximately 3 out of 10,000 children (National Academies of Sciences, Engineering, and Medicine (NASEM), 2015, p. 242). Since then, the diagnostic criteria for autism have been expanded to acknowledge the wide range of the spectrum (NASEM, 2015, p. 243). Other factors that have contributed to the increase in autism prevalence include:

- Improved diagnostic techniques, due to increased awareness of the autism spectrum and better screening of minority and low-income children, as well as women.
- A focus on early supports and interventions that are able to help improve deficits in critical areas, such as speech and self-care.
- An increase in diagnoses of previously undiagnosed adults – whose autism was missed in their younger years – who are now being recognized in adulthood. Many are diagnosed alongside their autistic children.

Broadly speaking, autism is characterized by issues with socialization, communication, and sensory input, but the way that these deficits manifest can vary wildly from person to person. Autism exists along a spectrum, but this spectrum is not a straight line from "low-functioning" to "high-functioning." More accurately, the autism spectrum can be thought of as being comprised of several gradients across a circle, similar to a color wheel.

Each color gradient represents a different aspect of autism: socialization, communication, perception, intelligence, self-help skills, etc. Any given individual with autism could be proficient in one area while underperforming in another. Ability levels can also vary from day-to-day, depending on a host of factors ranging from illness to sleep-deprivation to long-term stress levels. As a result, it can be enormously difficult to accurately pinpoint the level of need of a single autistic individual. For many, their needs can fluctuate over time. (For a more detailed explanation of the concept of the autism spectrum as a circle, see "Understanding the Spectrum," a web comic by autistic artist Rebecca Burgess.)

During my time as a special education teacher, the autistic children I taught came from a variety of diverse backgrounds: different races, classes, and genders. They each had distinct strengths and areas of need. They each had different interests and abilities. They each had varying levels of verbal communication. But one common thread that connected us all was storytelling.

THE IMPORTANCE OF LIBRARIES

Stories are one of the most powerful tools for working with autistic people. Stories can improve language and social development. Young people on the spectrum benefit from social stories – a selection of text paired with representative images – especially when these social stories explain and outline new experiences or ideas, such as going to school or riding a bus. Autistic individuals of all ages can spend hours engaged in their storytelling medium of choice: online videos, movies, television shows, cartoons, books, audiobooks, graphic novels, video games, and many others. An autistic mind is more likely to learn something new when it is presented in a concrete way – using real-life stories as examples, instead of metaphorical or symbolic representations. Stories can also help autistic people to better understand the world around them, and better understand themselves.

As repositories of stories, libraries can be powerful and empowering places for autistic children and adults. There are many library programs that can appeal to autistic patrons, and making these programs more sensory-friendly can lead to increased attendance numbers and better outcomes. By providing a safe and structured space for autistic individuals to exist in their local communities, libraries can create numerous opportunities for socialization and education that benefit both neurodivergent and neurotypical (nonautistic) patrons.

However, serving autistic patrons may be a relatively new concept for some libraries. Autistic children were mostly homebound or sent away to state institutions until the 1980s (Wright, 2015). The condition was not widely known in the 1990s and 2000s, aside from the controversy over a study that fraudulently linked autism to the measles–mumps–rubella vaccine (Godlee, Smith, & Marcovitch, 2011). While awareness of autism has increased over the past decade, this awareness has not necessarily given libraries and their staff the knowledge they need to effectively serve their autistic patrons (Okyle, 2015). Nevertheless, libraries nationwide have been diligently working to create inclusive environments and programming for autistic patrons.

Libraries and Autistic Children

Programming for autistic children is the typical starting point for libraries. Sensory storytimes are a natural extension of the read-alouds that libraries already offer. The addition of elements such as felt or flannel boards, hands-on objects or instruments, and repeating songs and chants are satisfying and beneficial to both neurodivergent and neurotypical patrons (Cottrell, 2016a).

Beyond specialized programming, libraries can also enrich the lives of their autistic patrons simply by being a place that is respectful of their differences. One of the most distinctive autistic traits in children is the use of self-stimulatory behavior – also known as "stimming" or "stims." An autistic individual may flap their hands, tap their fingers, or engage in countless other forms of movement. These stims serve a variety of functions, such as increasing focus while decreasing the severity of external sensory information. In other words, a child whose brain is having difficulty filtering out the sound of a humming overhead light may engage in certain actions, such as flicking their fingertips near their ears, in order to tune out the noise (Cottrell, 2016a). Stims may also be used when an autistic person is nervous, overwhelmed, or even happy.

Library staff members who are familiar with autistic traits can be excellent advocates and allies for autistic children. Their libraries become safe spaces where autistic children can observe the social behavior of others in their community, without fear of judgment or exclusion. Autistic children can use these social opportunities in the library space to utilize tools and strategies that will serve them in the world outside the library.

While many libraries are able to successfully implement sensory storytimes programs, the path to providing services to autistic adults is not always as straightforward. Libraries are more attuned to the needs of autistic children for two reasons: one, these children have advocates who can speak up on their behalf (usually their parent or guardian, but sometimes their sibling or another relative), and two, autistic children usually have more visible autistic traits.

Libraries and Autistic Adults

As they get older, autistic adults tend to improve their surface-level social skills and adopt subtler stimming behaviors. Their autism may be harder to spot, but they likely still struggle internally with navigating social interactions and regulating sensory stimuli. Libraries may find it more difficult to provide targeted services to these "invisible" autistics, especially when compared to the more visibly autistic children they serve (Cottrell, 2016b).

However, autistic adults are in desperate need of programming and services – especially those who have aged out of school-based programs (Okyle, 2015). The children who were diagnosed with autism under the expanded diagnostic criteria of the 1990s and 2000s are now adults, and the majority are no longer enrolled in school or post-secondary programs. Federally funded community programs for autistic adults are rare, and those that do exist have lengthy waiting lists – some of which are so long that schools have taken to advising parents to add their child's name to these waiting lists during their early elementary years. The result is a growing number of autistic adults who have come to depend on their libraries for socialization and educational opportunities. Offering programs similar to the Next Chapter Book Club (a book club for disabled teens and adults) or even a pop culture convention can give autistic adults a place to support their interests while also interacting with others in their community.

Libraries are discovering that they are inherently appealing to autistic adults for a multitude of reasons. Autistic adults find comfort in the stability and structure of the library. Libraries are fairly predictable places, with clearly-defined routines and rules. Many parts of the library experience can be accomplished with little direct social interaction, through the use of self-service kiosks for accessing catalogs and checking out materials. However, the work of the library staff still improves the library experience for autistic patrons, through the selection of new materials, the development of programming and events, and the comfort of seeing familiar faces in the building. Another benefit for autistic patrons is the fact that libraries are typically quiet spaces – and when they are not quiet, there is usually a justifiable reason for the noise.

Libraries also give autistic individuals access to one of their favorite things – technology. Technology has become a significant part of libraries, and it has become equally important to members of the autistic community (Zolyomi, 2018). Autistic individuals who have difficulty expressing themselves verbally or in writing may find success in typing or communicating through symbols (Asaro-Saddler, Knox, Meredith, & Akhmedjanova, 2015, pp. 106–107; Charlop-Christy, Carpenter, Le, Leblanc, & Kellet, 2002, p. 227). Some autistic individuals stim by listening to the same song or watching the same scene in a video over and over, and touchscreen devices make this action easy for even the youngest patrons. Technology can also be used to make connections and socialize. Faces, especially eyes, can be overwhelming to people on the spectrum, so communicating with friends via social media or over a headset can be easier for them (Hadjikhani et al., 2017; van Schalkwyk et al., 2017).

While libraries are not expected to meet every need of this population, they can make a powerful impact on the lives of the autistic adults in their communities. In return, these libraries can expect to gain loyal patrons, and perhaps even a future librarian.

SUPPORTING NEURODIVERSITY IN THE LIBRARY

Supporting Autistic Librarians

Autistic adults and the library profession are an understandable match. Autistic librarian Charlie Remy credits his interest in librarianship to three key factors: "early childhood exposure to public libraries, an extremely positive undergraduate library experience, and [a] love for information in all formats" (Eng, 2017). The same factors are likely to be found in many autistic adults. Patrons who have spent years in the library feel comfortable in the environment, and their analytical minds are especially adept at the skills needed to succeed and thrive in the field.

Supports for autistic employees in the library do not require enormous effort. Some simple supports that libraries can offer include:

- A structured and consistent routine with clear expectations.
- Written instructions or visuals of steps to complete a task.
- The option to wear high-fidelity earplugs or noise-canceling headphones.
- The ability to take a short break when overwhelmed.

Remy founded a Facebook group for "Autistics in Libraries and Their Allies" after he was unable to find an organization specifically dedicated to autistic librarians, but he hopes that the ALA and other groups will create their own initiatives to attract neurodivergent librarians in the future (Eng, 2017). Remy has also worked with the Massachusetts Library System to create a LibGuide on serving patrons and library employees with autism (Remy, 2019). Autistic librarians like Remy have insights that can be incredibly valuable to libraries looking to attract and support autistic employees.

Strategies for Autism-friendly Libraries

One of the best ways to improve services to autistic patrons is to hire autistic employees and librarians. Allowing autistic employees to develop and implement library programming for autistic patrons is akin to supporting the #OwnVoices literature movement (a hashtag that was, uncoincidentally, created by autistic author Corinne Duyvis). Representatives of a specific group have a unique understanding of the needs of others similar to themselves. Libraries seeking to hire autistic library staff and librarians can implement outreach programs to recruit and support autistic volunteers, interns, and employees. Libraries should also ensure that their entire library staff is trained in serving autistic patrons. While great progress has been made in this area, there is still much to be done, as evidenced by occasional incidents in which an autistic patron is asked to leave the library for stimming (Yorio, 2018).

Neurotypical library staff can still be indispensable advocates for autistic patrons. By learning more about the experiences of their autistic patrons, library staff can create respectful and autism-friendly libraries. Some key strategies to consider include:

- creating a dedicated quiet space;
- making detailed maps of the library available online;
- increasing signage in the library (with both text and images);
- including details about programming and events on the library website; and
- creating sensory kits for patron use.

Sensory kits can include items such as fidgets, noise-canceling headphones, and other sensory aids. The staff at the Deerfield Public Library allow patrons to access sensory kits from multiple locations – the front desk, the youth services desk, and the adult services desk – and patrons do not have to ask for permission to use the items (Sadin, 2018). These kits are available to anyone in the library. This and the other strategies detailed above are all ideas that benefit more than just the autistic patrons in the library. Just as elements of Universal Design – such as curb cuts, motion-activated sensors, Velcro, etc. – have improved the lives of both disabled and nondisabled citizens, the same is true of many autism-friendly library initiatives.

CONCLUSION

Libraries are vital places for the autistic community, so it is imperative that we continue to support our public libraries while simultaneously improving services for autistic patrons. Librarians, at their core, are driven to be passionate advocates for their patrons, so libraries should work to ensure that all library staff members are trained to support autistic patrons. Having a well-trained, empathetic library staff will benefit all patrons. As we continue our work in this area, it is important to note that one of the best ways to train staff is to share stories. Library staff members need to hear stories of grateful parents and happy kids who benefited from sensory storytimes. They need to hear the real-life experiences and ideas of autistic adults. They need to know what to expect from autistic patrons, so they can be prepared with strategies to appropriately and respectfully respond. They need to learn about what works, so they can bring new ideas to their own libraries to meet the needs of the autistic patrons in their community.

Librarian Barbara Klipper, a parent of autistic children, knows firsthand the difference that a great library can make: "Miracles can happen and it's not about the numbers … individual lives can be changed by these programs" (Foerster, Pelich, & Schriar, 2017, p. 17). Miracles do happen in our public libraries, because our libraries have something that no book store or warehouse could ever match – amazing, passionate, and brilliant library staff.

REFERENCES

American Library Association (ALA). (2019). Social impact|Libraries matter. Retrieved from http://www.ala.org/tools/research/librariesmatter/category/social-impact

Asaro-Saddler, K., Knox, H. M., Meredith, H., & Akhmedjanova, D. (2015). Using technology to support students with autism spectrum disorders in the writing process: A pilot study. *Insights into Learning Disabilities, 12*(2), 103–119. Retrieved from https://eric.ed.gov/?id=EJ1088270

Charlop-Christy, M. H., Carpenter, M. H., Le, L., Leblanc, L. A., & Kellet, K. (2002). Using the picture exchange communication system (PECS) with children with autism: Assessment of PECS acquisition, speech, social-communicative behavior, and problem behavior. *Journal of Applied Behavior Analysis, 35*(3), 213–231. https://doi.org/10.1901/jaba.2002.35-213

Cottrell, M. (2016a, March 1). Storytime for the spectrum. *American Libraries.* Retrieved from https://americanlibrariesmagazine.org/2016/03/01/sensory-storytime-spectrum-libraries-add-services-for-children-with-autism/

Cottrell, M. (2016b, April 29). Aging out of sensory storytime. *American Libraries.* Retrieved from https://americanlibrariesmagazine.org/2016/04/29/libraries-autism-services-aging-sensory-storytime/

Edwards, J. B., Rauseo, M. S., & Unger, K. R. (2011). Community centered: 23 reasons why your library is the most important place in town. *Public Libraries, 50*(5), 42–47.

Eng, A. (2017). Neurodiversity in the library: One librarian's experience. *The Asperger/Autism Network.* Retrieved from https://www.aane.org/neurodiversity-library-one-librarians-experience/

Foerster, P., Pelich, M., & Schriar, S. (2017). *Libraries partnering to serve the autism community: National forums offer direction,* White Paper. Retrieved from https://www.cyberdriveillinois.com/departments/library/libraries/pdfs/targeting-autism-whitepaper.pdf

Godlee, F., Smith, J., & Marcovitch, H. (2011). Wakefield's article linking MMR vaccine and autism was fraudulent. *British Medical Journal, 342*, 7452. https://doi.org/10.1136/bmj.c7452

Hadjikhani, N., Åsberg Johnels, J., Zürcher, N. R., Lassalle, A., Guillon, Q., Hippolyte, L., ... Gillberg, C. (2017, June 9). Look me in the eyes: Constraining gaze in the eye-region provokes abnormally high subcortical activation in autism. *Scientific Reports*, *7*, 3163. https://doi.org/10.1038/s41598-017-03378-5

National Academies of Sciences, Engineering, and Medicine (NASEM). (2015). Prevalence of autism spectrum disorder. In T. F. Boat & J. T. Wu (Eds.), *Mental disorders and disabilities among low-income children* (pp. 241–266). Washington, DC: The National Academies Press. https://doi.org/10.17226/21780

Okyle, C. (2015, Oct 31). Almost adult, with autism. *School Library Journal*. Retrieved from https://www.slj.com/?detailStory=almost-adult-with-autism

Remy, C. (2019). Services for patrons and employees on the autism spectrum. *Massachusetts Library System*. Retrieved from https://guides.masslibsystem.org/autism

Robison, J. E. (2013, October 7). What is neurodiversity? *Psychology Today*. Retrieved from https://www.psychologytoday.com/us/blog/my-life-aspergers/201310/what-is-neurodiversity

Sadin, S. (2018, November 7). As part of ongoing accessibility effort, Deerfield Library offers sensory kits. *The Chicago Tribune*. Retrieved from https://www.chicagotribune.com/suburbs/deerfield/ct-dfr-library-sensory-kits-tl-1115-story.html

TheDigitalArtist. (2016, October 17). *Colour wheel spectrum rainbow* [Digital image]. Retrieved from https://pixabay.com/illustrations/colour-wheel-spectrum-rainbow-1740381/

van Schalkwyk, G. I., Marin, C. E., Ortiz, M., Rolison, M., Qayyum, Z., McPartland, J. C.,... Silverman, W. K. (2017). Social media use, friendship quality, and the moderating role of anxiety in adolescents with autism spectrum disorder. *Journal of Autism and Developmental Disorders*, *47*(9), 2805–2813. https://doi.org/10.1007/s10803-017-3201-6

Wright, J. (2015, December 9). The missing generation. *Spectrum News*. Retrieved from https://www.spectrumnews.org/features/deep-dive/the-missing-generation/

Wright, J. (2018, December 3). National surveys estimate U.S. autism prevalence at 1 in 40. *Spectrum News*. Retrieved from https://www.spectrumnews.org/news/national-surveys-estimate-u-s-autism-prevalence-1-40/

Yorio, K. (2018, April 19). Incident offers opportunity for education on serving patrons with autism. *School Library Journal*. Retrieved from https://www.slj.com/?detailStory=incident-offers-opportunity-education-patrons-autism

Zolyomi, A. (2018, June 4). *Social connections for #ActuallyAutistic Adults* [PowerPoint slides]. Washington, DC: The University of Washington. Retrieved from http://depts.washington.edu/lend/trainees/project/2018/index.html

SECTION 4

THE FUTURE IS WAITING

CHAPTER 12

SYNERGISTIC COLLABORATION IN PUBLIC LIBRARIES: BUILDING BRIDGES IN THE ASIAN AMERICAN COMMUNITY TO CELEBRATE APIA HERITAGE MONTH

Jerry Dear

ABSTRACT

National cultural heritage months often highlight superficial elements such as food, arts, crafts, and music, but behind these celebrations lie generations of pioneers who have shaped the historical and cultural heritage of America. Over the past seven years, in championing cultural awareness, the San Francisco Public Library has collaborated with the Asian American Studies Department at San Francisco State University, The Association of Chinese Teachers, and other community organizations to commemorate Asian Pacific Islander American (APIA) Heritage Month every year in May. This annual program illustrates how efforts led by APIAs have contributed to the historical, cultural, and literary landscape of America, affording them the recognition they deserve. Multicollaborative efforts led to the creation of a premiere APIA Biography Project (apiabiography.sfsu.edu) – a digital repository of instructional resources that educators across the nation can adapt to their curriculum. By bridging collaboration, public engagement, and community partnerships,

Hope and a Future: Perspectives on the Impact that Librarians and Libraries Have on our World
Advances in Librarianship, Volume 48, 113–121
Copyright © 2021 by Emerald Publishing Limited
All rights of reproduction in any form reserved
ISSN: 0065-2830/doi:10.1108/S0065-283020210000048012

public libraries unify multiple constituencies to educate the public on the diverse communities they serve.

Keywords: Asian Americans; Asian Pacific American Heritage Month; Asian Pacific Americans; public libraries (San Francisco); cultural heritage months; ethnic heritage months

Community signifies a capstone element that resides at the heart of society, one that holds everything together. In today's world, public libraries function as one of the last remaining hubs of community building and resource sharing in society. Expanding on a previous article "Asian American Studies and The Association of Chinese Teachers Meet the Public Library" (Dear, 2018), this chapter examines how the San Francisco Public Library has raised cultural awareness for the Asian American community in honor of Asian Pacific Islander American (APIA) Heritage Month every year in May. Through a multicommunity partnership with the Asian American Studies (AAS) Department at San Francisco State University (SFSU), The Association of Chinese Teachers (TACT), the Square and Circle Club, and other community organizations, the library has emerged as a nexus that fosters collaborative engagement to celebrate this annual event by highlighting significant achievements APIAs have contributed to the social and cultural development of America.

APIA HERITAGE MONTH

The origin of APIA Heritage Month dates back to 1978 when President Jimmy Carter signed a Congressional joint resolution into law to designate one week to commemorate Asian/Pacific Americans as a recognized community in the United States (Library of Congress et al., n.d.). This legislation was spurred in part by capital staff member Jeanie F. Jew, also a board member of the Organization of Chinese Americans, who advocated for APIA community recognition by the US government amid nationwide advocacy campaigns during the mid-1970s:

> Ms. Jew was frustrated that Asian Pacific Americans were not included as a recognized community in the celebration of the United States Bicentennial and she would like to see the United States government acknowledge Asian Pacific Americans as part of the country. In addition, she also wanted to commemorate her great grand father [*sic.*] who had worked as a labor in the building of the Transcontinental Railroad. (APA Heritage Foundation, n.d.)

In 1990, President George W. Bush extended the duration of this heritage celebration to one month. 2018 marked the 40th anniversary of this month alongside other cultural heritage months such as Black History Month (February) and Hispanic Heritage Month (September/October).

THE APIA BIOGRAPHY PROJECT

The genesis of the APIA Biography Project (*apiabiography.sfsu.edu*) stemmed from an elective class in the AAS Department at SFSU. AAS 512 (formerly AAS 502) – Asian American Children's/Adolescent Literature – presents a survey of Asian American youth literature through concept books, picture books, chapter books, and young adult novels. The first of its kind in the nation, this class, designed and developed by Professor Lorraine Dong and later joined by Lecturer Jeannie Woo to teach a second section of this class, introduces students to the history and evolution of these works for youth (Dong & Woo, n.d.). Literature, or for that matter, film, television, and other forms of mass and social media impact young minds through popular culture, for they inevitably shape and mold perceptions of their identity in relation to others in a social context. This class accomplishes dual goals: First, students gain a historical and critical overview of Asian American youth literature through common literary themes, tropes, social issues, and stereotypes. Second, students produce curricular content – often tied to a specific theme – to showcase during APIA Heritage Month in the community. Afterwards, the educational materials are incorporated into a national database of curricular materials that K-12 educators can use for lesson planning and curriculum development. Since many history textbooks fail to address the accomplishments of marginalized groups including Asian Americans, this clearinghouse supplements a more culturally relevant curriculum in filling critical gaps in the annals of American history.

INAUGURAL APIA BIOGRAPHY PROJECT EVENT

Constituents of the first APIA Biography Project held a groundbreaking event in 2013 at the Merced Branch of the San Francisco Public Library. This event raised cultural awareness of APIA Heritage Month to San Francisco and the community at large. Although branch libraries tend to have smaller spaces, this branch included a courtyard area where tables were arranged for a series of outdoor hands-on learning activities. Inside the library, TACT educators set up tables to showcase their signature curricular guide *Crossing Boundaries: Asian & Pacific Islander Americans* (Collier, Collier, & Macbeth, 2010). This coloring booklet highlights distinguished APIA biographical portraits, including people such as horticulturist Lue Gim Gong, former queen of the kingdom of Hawai'i Lili'uokalini, Olympic diver Greg Louganis, champion golfer Tiger Woods, and many others. Several students in the AAS program at SFSU researched, wrote, and presented highlights of a prominent APIA individual as one of their course assignments. Since this class examines Asian American children's literature, the challenge required deciding which aspects of the subject's life to highlight, crafting a synopsis to match the reading level of a child, and illustrating a portrait of the individual, thereby adopting the complex method that children's writers and illustrators undertake to create works for young readers. This inaugural event launched a partnership that has continued to the present day, reinforcing a concerted effort shared by all through mutual confluence. Through AAS 512 – Asian American Children's/Adolescent Literature – students gained knowledge through a service-learning-based approach: They learned about Asian American history and culture through the lens of youth literature, utilized the library's resources in their research, designed and developed instructional materials with educators, presented their work in the community, and shared their products for future generations. The following sections offer an overview of the varied themes and topics.

APIAs ON THE STREETS – MAIN LIBRARY

In 2014, the main branch of the San Francisco Public Library provided a much larger venue, and during the second year, this event focused on streets and public spaces in San Francisco named after APIAs. Titled *A San Francisco Treat: Asian Pacific Islander Americans on the Streets*, over 30 locations were located and identified, covering a spectrum of community landmarks such as the Alice Fong Yu Alternative School in the Sunset district, Him Mark Lai branch library in Chinatown, Victoria Manaolo Draves Park in the South of Market Filipino American community, and the national headquarters of the Japanese American Citizens League in Japantown. The centerpiece of this event featured a large map of San Francisco: Labeled on this map were various stars, each one pinpointing a specific street or public space in the city; lines stretched outwards from each star to a captioned photo explaining the history and relevance of the site. The library furnished a versatile community meeting room that accommodated multiple learning activity tables, poster session displays, interactive games such as a Jeopardy style grid board projected onto a portable television screen, a storytelling corner for young children, a coloring book station, and much more. A long table of books stationed at the back of the room displayed numerous books written by and about APIAs, many of which could be checked out from the library. Students, college faculty, and schoolteachers worked in collaboration with each other to set up the room, and a media team was available to support the learning activities and looping slide presentations as needed.

APIA WOMEN BREAKING HISTORY

In the spirit of uncovering hidden and suppressed histories, in 2015 the APIA Biography Project shifted in another direction, turning the spotlight onto APIA women. Entitled "APIA Women Breaking History," this event featured how women shattered stereotypes reinforced by the mainstream media. A Wall of Fame located at the front of the room displayed 32 biographical portraits created by students in AAS 512, spotlighting women such as sculptor and artist Ruth Asawa, activist and writer Grace Lee Boggs, astronaut Kalpana Chawla, and state legislator Velma Veloria.

The library replicated this event in March 2016 in conjunction with national Women's History Month. Joining this collaborative effort was The Square and Circle Club (http://www.squareandcircleclub.org) – the first and oldest Chinese and Asian American women's service organization in the United States. Renamed to "APIA Women Making History," not only did this event debunk perpetual stereotypes of these women often portrayed in subservient roles (e.g., immigrant prostitutes, geisha concubines), but it highlighted the achievements they made in American history. Highlights of this event included the following: The San Francisco History Center, which had already archived artifacts from the Square and Circle Club, curated a showcase of the organization's memorabilia such as newspaper clippings, photos, letters, and a 75th anniversary program guide. The Magazines and Newspapers Center along with the Chinatown Branch Library compiled images of APIA women appearing on the covers of selected mainstream and independent magazines. The array of women featured personalities such as comedian and television star Margaret Cho (*Hyphen*), journalist Connie Chung (*Jade*), Nancy Kwan posing in her signature cheongsam as Suzie Wong (*Life Magazine*), and actress Ming Na Wen (*A. Magazine*). As usual, a separate table displayed books written by and about APIA women where attendees could also obtain a recommended reading list vetted and compiled by TACT educators.

BIOGRAPHICAL HIGHLIGHTS IN APIA HISTORY

The summer of 2016 marked the 130th anniversary of the Summer Olympics and as such, the thematic title for that year was "APIA Olympians Shooting for Gold." Biographical profile projects from both sections of AAS 512 included tennis player Michael Chang, Paralympian wheelchair racer Anjali Forber-Pratt, weightlifter Tommy Kono, and world-renowned figure skaters Michelle Kwan and Kristi Yamaguchi. The library supplemented the event with photos, articles, and digital images from the periodical archives, current magazine collection, and research databases. TACT also pooled their efforts to design learning activities to highlight the biographies of APIA Olympians.

In light of trending immigrant issues permeating the news and media in 2017, the spotlight shifted to a historical focus on APIA immigrants, highlighting early pioneers who arrived in America via Angel Island with the program – "American? Angel Island Immigrant Voices." This event, in collaboration with the Angel Island Immigration Station (*https://www.aiisf.org*), employed an immigration motif whereby children could embark on a simulated journey to migrate to America. By visiting different table stations, they made decisions regarding what to pack for the journey, obtained a passport, traveled overseas, and wrote to their families back home after having landed in America. Through these thematic activities, they could experience the immigration process and better understand the plight many immigrants faced in being uprooted from their homelands, reflecting the contemporary experiences of present-day immigrants. The Magazines and Newspapers Center collaborated with other library departments to compile newspaper articles that elucidated the history of the Angel Island Immigrant

Station, photos from the San Francisco Historical Photograph Collection, and book cover images from the library's children's and adult collections.

In the last couple of years (2018–2019), historical milestones advanced to the forefront of the APIA Biography Project, exploring political and social forces that contextualized APIAs in the American history narrative. For example, 2019 marked the 150th anniversary of the construction of the Transcontinental Railroad, a pivotal event in US history. In addition to highlighting the railroad workers and miners, this event – titled "APIAs Building Railroads across America" – showcased the contributions of pioneering APIAs who developed and transformed the modern transportation industry. In a standard American history curriculum, little information save for a paragraph attributes the role that immigrant gold miners and railroad workers played in building the nation's transportation infrastructure, so this event illuminated an integral chapter in American history. By developing the curriculum one year in advance, educators could adopt this content into their lesson plans for the following year. The library compiled an annotated resource list of news articles, historical photos, picture books, and history books. Furthermore, attendees at this event received an activity workbook that included a map of the railroads built by the Chinese up to 1870, logos of the railroad companies, and profiles of early notable Chinese railroad workers.

Moving forward, 2019 marked the 50th anniversary of the founding of ethnic studies and by extension AAS in the United States, leading to the next program – "APIAs Waking Up! Jump into Action." Half a century ago, sparked in part by San Francisco State College (now SFSU), this movement represented a mobilized effort by students to demand a culturally relevant curriculum. In short, they sought to reclaim their histories that had been omitted from the textbooks. The active groups comprised of marginalized students from Black, Latino/Hispanic, Native American, and Filipino and Asian American communities to reform the face of higher education across the nation – a monumental effort that endures to this day as ethnic studies leads the fight on contentious debates in public education. Embodying a form of social activism at its core, this event featured a Wall of Fame to honor the pioneering efforts of activists who led this grassroots resistance for a more comprehensive and authentic history, one that remains virtually absent from the standard American history curriculum today. Student members of the Intercollegiate Chinese for Social Action included Jeffery Paul Chan, Laureen Chew, Irene Dea Collier, and Malcolm Collier. Historians such as Him Mark Lai, christened the dean of Chinese American Studies, and Philip P. Choy joined forces to co-teach the first Chinese American course in the nation using their own text *A History of the Chinese in California: A Syllabus* (Chinn, Lai, & Choy, 1969). Student members of Pilipino American Collegiate Endeavor Danielo Begonia, Daniel Phil Gonzales, and Juanita Tamayo Lott led the Filipino American contingency in solidarity with other Asian groups. Another section also featured the early colleges that offered AAS classes in their curriculum. The Magazines and Newspapers Center of the Main Library presented an array of news article clippings and photos covering the ethnic studies movement from its origins in the late 1960s to the current day, as this discipline continually faces opposition as a general education requirement for high school students in California. As with the

Transcontinental Railroad program, participants received an activity book that highlighted Asian American pioneers who participated in the strike of 1968–1969 at SFSU, Asian American community student groups, a listing of colleges and universities offering Asian American Studies programs, an ethnic studies maze summarizing key events from 1968 to 2019, and other educational activities.

SERENDIPITOUS NETWORKING

Amid San Francisco Public Library's APIA events, networking opportunities emerged as a result of the library's efforts in connecting with the community. In 2018, the Mayor's APA Heritage Celebration Committee in San Francisco's City Hall was gearing up to celebrate the 40th anniversary of APIA Heritage Month and was formulating strategies to promote this landmark event. This community tradition, inaugurated by San Francisco Mayor Gavin Newsom in 2005, consisted of diverse community groups to coordinate this annual celebration. Executive director Stephen Gong from the Center for Asian American Media (CAAM, *https://caamedia.org*), a public media and cultural nonprofit organization in San Francisco, represented one of the constituencies of this planning committee. Recognizing the library's track record of community engagement in presenting Asian American-related programs, he invited the library to participate in this unique partnership. Joining other community partners such as the Asian Art Museum and the Asian Pacific Fund, this conglomerate group focused on achieving a singular purpose: Not only did this committee from the Mayor's office seek to raise awareness of this national heritage month throughout the city, but as a long-term ambitious goal, establish San Francisco as a cultural beacon for the entire nation. San Francisco, after all, represents a historical landmark and premiere destination where early Asian American immigrants arrived over 150 years ago, and they eventually settled in America as their permanent home.

In addition to joining as a community partner, the library also cultivated additional partnerships in the process. For example, every year in March, the CAAM hosts the "world's largest showcase for new Asian American and Asian film, food, and music program" in the United States (*https://caamedia.org/caamfest*). In 2017, CAAM decided to hold this annual festival in May to align with APIA Heritage Month in conjunction with other community organizations. Given that the library was already hosting over 200 programs across its 28 libraries throughout the city, it was a natural fit as a potential partner. Consequently, the main branch of the San Francisco Public Library joined CAAM's annual film festival (CAAMFest) in 2018, serving as a venue for one of the screenings at this festival. Unbeknownst to many patrons, the library has a 200-seat auditorium that serves as a public space for author lectures, musical performances and plays, open forums, and of course film screenings. In this first-year collaboration, the library co-presented *Power in Unity* – a selection of short documentaries examining the local urban housing crisis, focusing on Chinese seniors fighting displacement and seeking social justice for secure housing in San Francisco. In the second year (2019), the library hosted a special 20th anniversary screening of director

Deann Borshay Liem's *First Person Plural*. This film illuminates Liem's personal Korean American adoptee narrative, many of which remain largely unknown. Incidentally, the closing film of CAAMFest 2019 also featured her latest film *Geographies of Kinship*, revealing even more stories on the lived experiences of young adoptees from South Korea.

SYNERGISTIC CONNECTIONS AND BEYOND

Dr. S. R. Ranganathan's Fifth Law of Library Science states: "The Library is a growing organism" (Ranganathan, 2019). No more is this truer than in this age of information where people are both physically and digitally connected. Libraries have evolved beyond serving as mere vast repositories of information. Instead, they function as the nexus of a community hub, championing free and equitable access to information. Director and writer Emilio Estevez (2018) asserted this ideal in his film *The Public*: "The public library is the last bastion of democracy in America." The San Francisco Public Library has applied this principle through its perennial APIA Heritage Month program every year in May.

By forging partnerships with the AAS Department at SFSU, TACT, the Square and Circle Club, the Angel Island Immigration Station, and other organizations and institutions, the library has strategically positioned itself to serve its community in raising awareness of the diverse populations it supports as promulgated in its mission statement: "The San Francisco Public Library system is dedicated to free and equal access to information, knowledge, independent learning and the joys of reading for our diverse community" (*https://sfpl.org/about-us/library-administration*). Furthermore, these programs foster internal collaboration within its departments across multiple subject areas and disciplines to highlight unique collections, resources, and services, demonstrating that individual departments need not always operate in silos, but instead, combine their efforts to host programs for all ages. In fact, the Angel Island Immigrant Voices program attracted attention, so much so that the Richmond Branch of the San Francisco Public Library replicated a scaled-down version of the event. Educators who attended received an educational toolkit they could adopt into their respective schools in the local community. Not only did this event transform into a professional development opportunity for educators, but it also attracted parents and families in another neighborhood of the city who rarely visit the Main Library due to its remote location.

Most importantly, the continued success of the APIA Biography Project over the past seven years demonstrates a need to offer a much larger spotlight on diverse communities in connection with national heritage months, and to do so in a manner that reflects their accomplishments with sensitivity, respect, and authenticity. Many cultural events focus on superficial aspects of ethnic groups through activities such as food, arts, crafts, and music. While these efforts shed light on these communities, the APIA Biography Project aims to magnify the unique contributions of individuals who played historical and impactful roles culminating in the cultural and social construction of America. By positioning itself as a strategic partner with various organizations and city agencies, then, the San Francisco Public Library has forged synergistic collaborations, demonstrating that libraries do, in fact, function as growing organisms that thrive by transcending traditionally held roles, impacting their communities and beyond. In navigating this trajectory, public libraries symbolize a beacon of persistent hope in our communities, educational institutions, and the country as a whole, thereby honoring, upholding, and preserving the deeper truths of America as a nation of immigrants.

REFERENCES

APA Heritage Foundation. (n.d.). *Origin of Asian Pacific American heritage month.* Retrieved from https://apasf.org/history

Chinn, T. W., Lai, H. M., & Choy, P. P. (Eds.). (1969). *A history of the Chinese in California: A syllabus.* San Francisco, CA: Chinese Historical Society of America.

Collier, I. D., Collier, L. M., & Macbeth, J. (2010). *Crossing boundaries: Asian & Pacific Islander Americans.* San Francisco, CA: The Association of Chinese Teachers. Retrieved from https://tinyurl.com/rhv32qc

Dear, J. (2018). Asian American studies and the association of Chinese teachers meet the public library: A multi-community approach to planning APIA programs. In J. H. Clarke, R. Pun, & M. Tong (Eds.), *Asian American librarians and library services: Activism, collaborations, and strategies* (pp. 135–139). Lanham, MD: Rowman & Littlefield.

Dong, L., & Woo, J. (n.d.). *APIA biography project.* Retrieved from http://apiabiography.sfsu.edu

Estevez, E. (Director). (2018). *The public* [Film]. Universal City, CA: Universal Pictures Home Entertainment.

Library of Congress, National Archives and Records Administration, National Endowment for the Humanities, National Gallery of Art, National Park Service, Smithsonian Institution, & United States Holocaust Memorial Museum. (n.d.). *Asian Pacific American heritage month.* Retrieved from https://asianpacificheritage.gov/about

Ranganathan, S. R. (2019). *The five laws of library science.* University of Southern California Library. Retrieved from https://tinyurl.com/ya5l47x9

CHAPTER 13

A VOICE OF HOPE: SERVING THROUGH DIGITIZATION AND INITIATIVE

Jaime Valenzuela

ABSTRACT

In a field where external factors can far too easily define who we are as professionals, it is up to us to prove our worth. Even when a position appears to lack opportunity for advancement, we can earn recognition through hard work and initiative. In doing so, we invite other opportunities to come our way. This chapter will demonstrate how the author developed his niche as classified staff in the Daniel F. Cracchiolo Law Library at the James E. Rogers College of Law, University of Arizona. By showing initiative early and often, the author was afforded the opportunity to work on two important digitization projects at the library. The first project involved getting the scholarly work of students in the Indigenous Peoples Law and Policy Program represented in the campus repository. The second project involved supervising a Law Library Fellow's internship, which included resurrecting in-house digitizing equipment. In detailing these two undertakings, the author will demonstrate why libraries play an important role in digitization. Furthermore, the author will show how up-and-coming library professionals can demonstrate the power of the library, earn recognition, and set the stage for further professional opportunities.

Keywords: Digitization; initiative; collaboration; required standards; repository; internship

Hope and a Future: Perspectives on the Impact that Librarians and Libraries Have on our World
Advances in Librarianship, Volume 48, 123–132
Copyright © 2021 by Emerald Publishing Limited
All rights of reproduction in any form reserved
ISSN: 0065-2830/doi:10.1108/S0065-283020210000048013

Before I began working in libraries, I worked retail. My sense of self-worth was less than ideal. I wanted to offer something more valuable than the location of a sundry. It is a reason I chose to work in libraries. I thought I was leaving the mundane duties behind me, but mail processing was my primary responsibility when I started working at the Daniel F. Cracchiolo Law Library (Library). In time I was charged to do more at my library. As I hope this chapter shows, I helped create that opportunity through a good work ethic and a willingness to take advantage of my circumstances. There is an abundance of hardworking, knowledgeable information professionals who are still waiting for their opportunity to contribute on a broader scale. Such opportunities are possible. One need only consider their current position and discover how they can assist their institution.

I saw my opportunity in how I chose to handle my primary responsibility of processing incoming mail and via a vacant position in the Special Collections unit of the Technical Services Department in the Library. In two years, from an entry-level position started in February 2016, I demonstrated hard work, assumed additional responsibilities, and earned the trust of my supervisor. With my supervisor's trust in hand, I was charged with overseeing the digitization of the Indigenous Peoples Law and Policy (IPLP)[1] Doctor of Juridical Science (SJD) Program's student dissertations in collaboration with the University of Arizona's Campus Repository[2] in the summer of 2018. In the spring of 2018, I was also privileged to serve as a site supervisor for a digitization internship. In detailing both projects, this chapter will exhibit the numerous ways the library is important to digitization work, from quality control and metadata entry to providing open-access via collaboration. Both library projects allowed me to provide value at a scale the library consistently offers.

A CHANCE TO SHOW INITIATIVE

Mail Processing and the Vacant Position

When the position of Library Assistant Senior opened at the Library, I hoped other library school graduates viewed the position negatively as mail processing was the primary responsibility. A recent graduate of the University of Arizona's School of Library and Information Science Graduate Program and a Knowledge River Scholar,[3] I regarded the position as a foot-in-the-door at an academic library. In February 2016, I was offered the position and I accepted. My first desk was located near the loading dock of the Library where incoming mail for the James E. Rogers College of Law (College) was delivered.

When the buzzer located at the dock sounded, it was likely a delivery. On occasion, law school faculty expected their packages and would come down to retrieve it. The driver, the delivery person, and the mail processor were often nothing more than an afterthought unless there was a misunderstanding. Then there was a need to explain why an incoming package was delivered to the processing facility of the carrier and not the Library. Such misunderstandings allowed me to demonstrate my ability to navigate difficult situations, such as communicating with agitated law school faculty. I also promoted myself as a calm, problem-solving employee.

As the individual processing mail for the College, I became a familiar face. For a significant amount of time, my face was associated with the mail and mail only. I did my best to consider my association with the mail as an advantage. Even when I didn't, I used it to my advantage. If I handled the mail well, people around the college would appreciate my work. My supervisor would value me. My colleagues would respect me. The mail became a duty they did not have to worry about. Everyone knew the mail would be handled, and more importantly, they knew I was managing it. If the opportunity presented itself, I would hand-deliver packages to faculty and introduce myself. I used mail as a way to make myself known. How I managed my mail responsibilities was critical to where I find myself now and the opportunities I have been granted.

Shortly after starting my new position, I learned that the Library Specialist responsible for Special Collections and Archives at the Library would soon be vacating their position. I told my supervisor, the Head of Technical Services, that I was interested in working with special collections and that I had some knowledge in working with archival material. I informed them that I was willing to help assume any duties required of the position. My supervisor was appreciative of my willingness to help take on extra work if needed, and they granted me the opportunity to work with the Library Specialist before their departure. Over two or three meetings with the outgoing Library Specialist, I and two colleagues learned about Special Collections and Archives at the Library. Responsibilities included management of the ephemera collection, environmental monitoring, and handling research requests. After the Library Specialist's departure, I took it upon myself to accept any task related to Special Collections and Archives that I could. After several months, with the Library Specialist position still vacant and with my supervisor's support, I spoke with the Library Director and expressed my interest in assuming the responsibilities of the position permanently. In January 2017, I was promoted to Library Specialist, undertaking all responsibility for the duties associated with Special Collections. Mail processing remained my primary responsibility in the Library.

SHOWING SELF-WORTH IN COLLABORATION: WORKING WITH IPLP AND THE CAMPUS REPOSITORY

Project Background

My supervisor believed representation in the University of Arizona's Campus Repository would create a greater working relationship with the University Libraries. It would also increase the visibility of the College and support the practice of open access. The opportunity for the College to contribute to the Campus Repository presented itself in the summer of 2018. Wanting to get the IPLP SJD student-produced dissertations digitized and made available online for easy access, the IPLP Assistant Director came to the Library for help.

Current IPLP SJD students would often request to see examples of previous student work according to the IPLP Assistant Director. With a growing program, making the dissertations available online would benefit current student success and would aid in making IPLP SJD research available to a broader audience. My supervisor agreed to help. They mentioned the Campus Repository as an ideal place to store the dissertations for both access and reaching a greater audience. My supervisor informed me that I would be the point of contact for the Library on the IPLP digitization project.

As my supervisor explained at my annual review, they considered my completion of the project as my greatest achievement for that year. The project involved coordination with the IPLP Assistant Director, members of the Campus Repository, and adhering to a specific set of standards and best practices. It also led to the development of a workflow for future digitization projects the Library may undertake. My work on the project also set the groundwork for future collaborations with IPLP, the Campus Repository, and what the Library hopes will be other College of Law departments. My contribution to the project was the type of value I wanted to provide.

Standards Are Important

The importance of libraries in digitization work is outlined in the project tasks I was responsible for completing. In late July 2018, I learned of my tasks during the first collective meeting between all parties involved in the IPLP digitization project. The tasks were to: digitize the dissertations, adhere to the digitization standards outlined by the Campus Repository, enhance the digitized material by running Optimal Character Recognition (OCR), enter the required metadata, and deposit digitized material into the Campus Repository. The project work outlined was intricate, and my supervisor believed that my performance over the previous two years demonstrated my ability to complete it.

Anyone can digitize material. Not everyone can do it meeting required standards. The standards required by the Campus Repository for digitization, such as scanning black and white material at a resolution of 600 DPI and adhering to a Dublin Core metadata-based schema, represents why libraries are essential to digitization work. Without standards, the digitized material the Library produced may not provide an optimal viewing experience for anyone accessing the IPLP material in the future or provide the necessary metadata for the items to be discovered.

Upon request, I provided the IPLP Assistant Director the in-house call number to search the library's catalog so they could view which IPLP SJD dissertations may be available for digitization. After review, they provided me with their request to digitize all the dissertations we held in our collection (13 spiral-bound items). Next, a Campus Repository affiliate provided me with a list of required and optional metadata fields that my boss and I reviewed with feedback from the IPLP Assistant Director. We also took into account what IPLP SJD students would want to view when searching and accessing material online. The Director of Campus Repository Services stressed the importance of providing as much of a complete metadata record as possible. All collaborators agreed that if the information was available in the physical items, I would include descriptive and administrative[4] metadata for both the required and optional metadata fields.

To digitize at the required resolution and to preserve the physical material best as possible, I needed to research digitization options. Research included looking at digitization equipment, both in-house and out, and how to best digitize the physical material. Fortunately for me, another member of the Library staff had experience digitizing a significant amount of material with a previous employer. They provided guidance on the spiral binding and best practices for digitization. I opted to digitize the material by removing the spiral binding. As for the digitizing equipment, the library owned an Epson WorkForce DS-510 scanner[5] that could scan at a resolution of 600 DPI. I located the available product documentation online, and I used it to guide myself through the digitization process. I completed scanning in less than a week thanks to the abilities of the scanner, and unbound dissertations were rehoused in archival quality folders. For our preservation purposes, the material was scanned to output TIFFs as a "lossless format allows for high-quality images to be preserved" (Corrado & Sandy, 2014, p. 195).

To provide an accessible and searchable document, I used Adobe Acrobat DC to compile all images into individual PDFs and enhanced each document with OCR. After all images were compiled, I clicked through each page of the compiled PDF to verify pages were not missing. If there was a page missing, I rescanned the missing page and inserted it into the compiled PDF. With all pages accounted for, I then ran OCR. This process took less than a week. By early August, I was ready to upload the digitized material to the Campus Repository.

Following a few weeks of correspondence between all involved parties, I began uploading materials into the Campus Repository in October. I also entered the metadata that was required and discussed at our initial meeting. I encountered some issues with the metadata entry due to my lack of experience using the Campus Repository platform, but the issues were resolved with some assistance from the Director of the Campus Repository. I completed uploading the PDFs and adding metadata in November.

In February 2019, the material I uploaded became available via the Campus Repository. I informed my supervisor and they requested that I announce the news to the rest of the Library. I wrote an email detailing the project and sent it out to Cracchiolo Law Library staff on February 12, 2019. Among the praise I received in announcing the completion of the project was a note from the Cracchiolo Law Library Interim Director: reading, "Another way to show to the whole College the value of the law library staff!!" (S. Esposito, personal communication, February 14, 2019).

SERVING AS A SITE SUPERVISOR: COLLABORATION AT ITS FINEST

Law Library Fellows and Their Interest in Special Collections

At the Library, the Law Library Fellowship Program was founded in the year 2000 to mentor and produce law librarians.[6] Law Library Fellows are graduate students in the University of Arizona's School of Information who have already obtained a Juris Doctorate Degree and are pursuing a Master of Arts degree in

Library and Information Science. There are two to six Law Library Fellows working in the Library at any time during the year. Some express interest in working with special collections. The first opportunity I had to work with a Law Library Fellow came in the spring semester of 2018. Knowing the Law Library Fellow had no prior knowledge of archival work, I organized and planned out a semester's worth of introductions and hands-on experience in the hopes of providing an overview of special collections work at the Library. Upon completion of the project, the Law Library Fellow's supervisor, a librarian in the Public Services Department, described my supervision of the work as having exceeded expectations. They stated they could not have imagined how well the experience would turn out for the Law Library Fellow. My work with the Law Library Fellow further demonstrated my value to the library and extended me the opportunity to pass on my knowledge to another. I gained the trust of another colleague, and I showed that I was capable of devising a project and supervising one's work.

In the late spring of 2018, a different Law Library Fellow (Fellow) expressed interest in digitizing some of the Library's print material related to the Colorado River Compact. Furthermore, they wanted to learn to use the in-house digitizing equipment and make that digitized content available online. The Fellow's Supervisor reached out to my supervisor to see if such an internship would be possible. After a discussion with my supervisor, which included an inquiry about my comfort level to take on such responsibility, I said I was willing to supervise the Fellow and oversee the internship. It was another opportunity for me to extend value onto another.

A Digital Collections Internship: Value for Supervisor and Law Library Fellow

My first step in serving as a site supervisor was to write an internship description for the Fellow. I approached the internship description as a professional development opportunity for myself; it would be the first internship description I would write. I also wanted to ensure that the Fellow's initial hopes for the internship were captured. I drafted and shared the description with my supervisor, the Fellow's supervisor, and the Fellow seeking feedback in May 2018 (Fig. 1). The internship description demonstrated why libraries are essential to digitization work by highlighting the need to establish a procedure, gain insight into unknown processes, and to provide access to digitized materials. Positive feedback for the description was received, and it enabled the Law Library Fellow to describe the project work accurately. Though the feedback I received for the internship description was not particularly insightful, the act of sharing it established a collaborative process. Both for me and the Fellow, collaboration would prove to be the foundation for success. In July of 2018, the School of Information approved the internship.

I began to converse with the Fellow about the project work that same May. Their intellect and enthusiasm were apparent. Informally, the Fellow and I began to research the digitization equipment we had in-house, an Atiz BookDrive DIY v-shaped overhead scanner,[7] per the job description. The Fellow deduced that one of the cameras used to capture images was equipped with a broken lens, and they priced the cost of a replacement. I successfully found how-to-scan documentation

Digital Collections Intern

Job Description:

The Daniel F. Cracchiolo Law Library has digitized a number of our holdings to provide online access to various materials from the collection. The Law Library owns digitizing equipment, in particular a book scanner that has not been used for some time and is currently inoperative. The Law Library is seeking to make its digitizing equipment operable in the hopes of adding value to its digital collections. The digital collections intern will play an integral role in reestablishing the Law Library's digitization efforts and contribute to our digital collection under the supervision of the Library Specialist through the following duties:

Description of Work to be performed:

Evaluate the current condition of the Law Library's book scanner and investigate new digitizing equipment

- o Identify any issues including malfunctioning hardware or outdated software
- o Provide recommendations including estimates for repair and/or replacement of equipment and software
- o Gain a working knowledge of the current digitization equipment and software

Select material for digitization

- o In accordance with the Law Library's collection development policy, select material for digitization
- o Evaluate condition of material
- o Research established digitization workflows
- o Assist the Library Specialist in establishing a workflow for digitizing material (Develop an SOP)

Add material to Law Library Digital Collection

- o Gain a working knowledge of Omeka (Law Library's open-source web publishing platform)
- o Assist the Library Specialist in uploading digitized material with necessary metadata

Project Review

- o Summarize the project including positive and negative outcomes
- o Propose future digitization projects

Fig. 1. Digitization Internship Description.

online, which I hoped would inform the act of digitizing, and I retrieved purchasing information for the BookDrive. The rapport established between myself and the Fellow before the internship began allowed me to establish how I would approach the internship as a site supervisor.

I knew I wanted to be flexible and supportive given the support I have received from my Technical Services Supervisor. I told the Fellow that I would handle making all official requests, that I would review any questions they had promptly, and I would allow for flexibility in their schedule so long as work hours were completed during Library business hours. That flexibility allowed for an affable working relationship between the Fellow and myself.

In August 2018, the internship officially started. The Fellow took it upon themselves to keep a journal of their daily activities while interning. Journal entries included findings, general notes, and project work completed. Given the Fellows' initiative in starting their daily journal, I chose to set up a working folder in the Library's SharePoint account to keep track of all working documents associated with the project. The working folder also allowed my supervisor and the Fellow's Supervisor to remain abreast of the project work.

To help complete project work and best inform decisions, I set up several meetings early in the internship with professionals on the University of Arizona campus who worked with digital materials in both current and former positions. In those meetings, which both the Law Library Fellow and I attended, we were provided insight into digitization workflows, procedure documentation, digitizing equipment, and required metadata. The meetings provided us with valuable connections across the University, which may one day aid the Library in future digitization endeavors. Outside of my capacity as a site supervisor, I also worked on some projects that required the digitization of physical materials. To complete those projects, I requested that the Fellow use our BookDrive DIY to digitize that material. The Fellow and I agreed that their assistance in my project work would aid their ability to operate the digitization equipment successfully and would inform the operating procedure they were charged to help develop. The collaborative efforts described above both in project work and meetings may not be unique to libraries, but it does show why libraries are important to digitization work. The willingness to promote best practices, the sharing of information across organizations, and providing opportunities to learn while on the job make the library essential to digitization work.

The Fellow and I agreed that it would be in the Library's best interest to get the BookDrive working rather than replacing it with a newer model. A new lens was delivered in early September after an approved purchase request I submitted was made. The Fellow ensured the lens worked and began to familiarize themselves with the operation of the scanner and how to best capture images. In October, they started drafting an operating procedure that included insights into material assessment, equipment, and image control. After establishing some confidence in operating the digitization equipment through related project work, the Fellow needed material to digitize as outlined in the job description. I provided a list of subject headings for the Fellow to search.[8] After they concluded the search, we chose four items for digitization taking into account the following characteristics of the material: length, content, and physical condition. To aid in a successful digitization run the first time, I also made three recommendations based on book length, physical condition, and content. Of the three recommendations, the Fellow selected one to digitize first. In the next several months, the Fellow successfully digitized all four items.

Throughout the internship, I familiarized myself with the Omeka,[9] the Library's chosen web-publishing platform. Familiarization included looking at how-to videos via the Omeka Vimeo webpage and tinkering with the Omeka platform when logged in. Watching the online tutorials provided me with the knowledge to build digital collections and add individual items. The Fellow also familiarized themselves with Omeka, specifically the metadata associated with the Library's digital content. In reviewing that digital content, we discovered it was living on a locally hosted server,[10] which we were provided access to with help from my supervisor and the College's Information Technology Department. To provide access to the Library's digital content, an open-source tool called The BookReader[11] was used. Users were also directed to PDFs via hyperlinks embedded within individual item metadata created in Omeka. The Fellow reviewed The BookReader source code and determined where to manipulate it to read any newly created digital content. I located where in the metadata we could embed hyperlinks and shared any knowledge I developed about Omeka with the Fellow.

The operating procedure developed encompassed the entire digitization process, including simple steps such as turning on the cameras to more difficult ones such as modifying The BookReader source code to read captured images. The operating procedure also included the standards we established to digitize material. Standards included the need to capture images at a resolution of 600 DPI, saving image files as both TIFFs and JPGs, and moving all digital content to the locally hosted server. Challenges, including capturing blank pages and crashing software, were summarized in a software review by the Fellow. I provided suggestions when I could, and I allowed time for challenges to be solved. With the operating procedure complete, I informed the Law Library Fellow of where I felt there was a need to provide further and clearer instructions.

Once digitization was completed, I built a new digital collection.[12] The collection included all four items the Law Library Fellow digitized. I added the necessary metadata for the individual items with input from the Law Library Fellow, and we successfully embedded links within the metadata. The links provided access to the digital content via The BookReader and PDFs. With the project work complete, I sent out an email to Library personnel writing to the Fellow's accomplishments and announced the newly created digital collection. My supervisor replied to the announcement formally via email: reading:

> Getting the scanner back up and running is a great accomplishment. It was able to be restored at minimal expense, too .... I'm sure this will lead to us expanding our digital collections. Again, great job. Thanks to you both. (T. Spence, personal communication, January 25, 2019)

CONCLUSION

I chose to work in libraries because I wanted to provide value that would extend beyond a shopping cart. I am now doing so. Required standards, the quality of digital content produced, and how access to that content is provided make the library valuable to digitization. I am fortunate to have had a hand in producing such quality and access both individually and collaboratively. In adhering to required standards and serving as a supervisor, I provided the value I knew I was capable of. The library is full of opportunity and it is possible for anyone to contribute. With a little initiative, that opportunity will present itself to someone else soon and well into the future.

NOTES

1. For more information on the IPLP Program, visit https://law.arizona.edu/indigenous-peoples-law-policy.

2. For more information on the University of Arizona Campus Repository, visit https://repository.arizona.edu/.

3. As a Knowledge River Scholar, I am committed to the needs of Latino and Native American populations. For more information on the Knowledge River, see https://ischool.arizona.edu/knowledge-river.

4. For more information on descriptive and administrative metadata, see Corrado and Sandy (2014), especially Table 5.1 in chapter 5.

5. For more information on the Epson WorkForce scanner, visit https://epson.com/For-Home/Scanners/Document-Scanners/Epson-WorkForce-DS-510-Color-Document-Scanner/p/B11B209201.

6. For more information on the Law Library Fellows Program, visit http://lawlibrary.arizona.edu/about/fellows-program.

7. For more information on ATIZ scanners, visit https://www.atiz.com/.The model owned by the Cracchiolo Law Library is no longer being produced. It was purchased in 2011.

8. I provided the following search terms for the Law Library Fellow to search in the Cracchiolo Law Library's LSP Primo. Water Rights – Arizona, Colorado River Compact, Colorado River – Water Rights.

9. For more information on Omeka, visit https://www.omeka.net/.

10. In the summer of 2019, the Cracchiolo Law Library learned that the locally hosted server used to provide access to its digital content would no longer be supported. Digital content is now hosted via its University of Arizona Box account.

11. For more information on The BookReader, visit https://openlibrary.org/dev/docs/bookreader.

12. The Cracchiolo Law Library no longer uses The BookReader to provide access to its' digital content. To view material from the digital collection, The Colorado River Compact, visit https://ualawlib.omeka.net/collections/show/15.

REFERENCE

Corrado, E. M., & Sandy, H. M. (2014). *Digital preservation for libraries, archives, and museums.* New York, NY: Rowman & Littlefield.

CHAPTER 14

LIBRARIANS AND LIBRARIES AS TWENTY-FIRST CENTURY TRANSFORMERS

Angiah Davis

ABSTRACT

Libraries are staples of the community. Yet, libraries are threatened everyday with the possibility of losing even more funding for staffing, services, and programs, or closing indefinitely due to budget cuts and decision-makers not understanding the value of libraries and librarians and library staff. While there may be fewer libraries in the future, libraries are here to stay. However, the role of librarians and libraries are changing. Whereas before, the library was a quiet place to study, a place to check out books, and a place to participate in storytime, libraries of the twenty-first century are becoming the place for all things related to people and customer service. Twenty-first-century librarianship is a business about serving the people. For the library to sustain itself, it must be the center of the community. Librarians must understand this notion. Library leaders must work collaboratively with community partners and citizens to transform their thinking and exceed expectations of the community. This chapter will discuss the role of librarians and libraries as change agents. This chapter will also share real examples of effective programs and services, why these programs and services are important, and ways one may implement these program models at their library.

Keywords: Change agents; collaboration; community engagement; community partnerships; customer service; twenty-first century librarianship

Hope and a Future: Perspectives on the Impact that Librarians and Libraries Have on our World
Advances in Librarianship, Volume 48, 133–138
ISSN: 0065-2830/doi:10.1108/S0065-283020210000048014

THE ROLE OF LIBRARIANS AND LIBRARIES REDEFINED

What do artificial intelligence, gamification, and makerspaces have in common? The answer is the twenty-century library. Librarianship is a noble profession. Librarians help shape a campus and/or a community without the notoriety of a celebrity or an elected official. Libraries and librarians are resources for the community as well. Libraries and librarians have the potential to transform their communities in many positive ways. In some libraries we may serve as a counselor one day, a janitor the next day, or a security guard the next day. In other libraries we serve as storyteller, instructor, or research partner. Libraries are essential to the community. Libraries are trusted storehouses of information, and librarians are the superheroes. We help save the day for library users in distress. Effective twenty-first-century librarians are viewed as mobile resources and co-collabora- tors that create lifelong learners in the community. Librarianship in the twenty- first century is about meeting library users literally and figuratively. This means that librarians should conduct outreach so that people are aware of services and resources. Libraries should also provide programming that meets the needs of the community by exploring their communities by talking to people and visiting places. For example, public librarians might start with a local community group that meets in the library. Academic librarians might familiarize themselves with the campus and identify potential faculty and staff to serve as collaborators when executing campus library initiatives.

Libraries should also be places where the community can be exposed to new and interesting topics in a nonthreatening manner. While librarians are making impacts in their communities and on campuses, it is important that these are communicated to key decision-makers. Libraries are changing, so that means that librarians must change their thinking as well. For example, at one time a librarian's job description may have consisted of seven key things, but now it has evolved to 11 things in order to effectively and efficiently serve the community.

EXAMPLES AND SIGNIFICANCE

A few years ago, I worked in a small branch public library in an at-risk neighbor- hood in Atlanta, and a young African-American male came in to receive help with writing a paper. At the time, I was a paraprofessional in library school. I told the young man that the library does not provide that type of writing assistance services, but that today was his lucky day. I told him I was a writing consultant, a job I had while in college, and a communications major, and that since we were not that busy at the desk, I would be more than happy to come over to his table to assist him with his paper. He wanted someone to look over his college entrance essay. This was my exact job, in college, reading and reviewing essays for students. I looked over the document, gave him feedback, and he went on his way. I wished him well, and I did not think any more about it. You come to work, do your job, go home, and repeat the next day. About three and a half years later, I was working at another library, and to my surprise the young man came up to me, and asked if I remembered him. Of course, I didn't remember him! I help many people each day and often never have the opportunity to learn their names. The young man proceeded to tell me his name and said that I was the lady who helped him get into college. "I did?" I asked. "You did!" he replied. "Oh, yes, yes, yes! I do remember helping you that day," I responded excitedly. He stated that he was in his junior year at Morehouse College and that he was interested in becoming a neurosurgeon. He went on to share that thanks to me he got into college. I was both shocked and ecstatic. To think that I made an impact on this young man at one library, he remembered me when our paths crossed again at another library, and he thought to say "thank you." That is an impact story to me. This story speaks volumes, and I will never forget it. I just helped the young man because I could even though I knew that was not part of my job description. This is what I am passionate about, helping people achieve their goals. At the public library I encounter all types of people from all walks of life daily. Some are looking for jobs. Some are seeking books on business plans. Some are interested in beginning their future. As a librarian, I make myself available to assist where needed. Perhaps, I will run into this young man again at another library where he will share news of his entry into medical school.

Another example of a small act making a huge impact is the time I met an elementary school student who wanted to start a book club in the community for girls ages 7–14. "What a great idea," I told the student and her mother. The student created a name for the book club, a logo, bylaws, activities, a flyer, a shirt for the girls to wear, and recruited members. The book club is held once a month at the library. This program encourages girls to read. The program also allows girls to develop social skills and demonstrates leadership and entrepreneur ability. The founder of the book club said that I, the librarian, was making her dream come true. What an inspiration! I did two things: Provided a space for the student to carry out her plan and promoted the program. The library is a place where patrons can make their dreams happen. Something that seems so small can actually have a huge impact on the patron and the community.

Have you ever had to help someone type a resume who has little to no computer skills? This happened to me, and the person got the job. The patron wanted to pay me for my work. Of course, I did not take the money, but it made me proud knowing that I was able to teach someone with little to no computer skills how to find and apply for a job in the twenty-first century. As a result, the branch has partnered with an employment agency with a main goal of providing information about work programs and services to the library patrons and the community at large. Twice a week beginning in March, representatives from the employment agency will be on site at the library to provide information about employment and job training services. By partnering with this agency, the branch is helping patrons find jobs and also providing a direct referral source to another county agency for those residents in need of participation in programs and services.

There are many more stories that I could share. Like the story about a library staff member who received a scholarship for their child to attend college by attending a financial aid workshop. The library hosted a few financial aid workshops for high school students and their parents. These workshops were free and conducted by a representative from the Georgia Student Finance Commission. Parents and students learned about the financial aid process, how to apply for financial aid, including scholarships. This is a great example of a financial literacy program and how the library not only helps patrons but helps staff as well.

A partnership with a local high school will allow students to display their high-quality original artwork in the branch. Art work will be displayed for a month and will change out every month. The purpose of this project is to support our local high school students by offering them the opportunity to publicly showcase their work. The partnership will also provide additional eye-catching artwork for the branch. We are committed to serving the community and having community artwork on display inside the branch, particularly by our local teens, is an honor. Teens may feel proud of their work and bring in family and friends to see their work displayed in the branch.

Learning should be fun. What better way is there to learn something new or reinforce something you already know than through gaming? Most people like to play games. Games are fun. Games have purpose. Games are for everyone. Hence, the reason academic librarians held International Games Day (IGD) at the Library. IGD has turned into International Games Week which is held annually in November to connect communities to their library through games. During IGD, students, faculty, and staff were invited to the library to play games with library staff and enjoy snacks. The library provided space for fun and educational activities. The social interaction with library staff, faculty, and students created a sense of community. One student told us that "[IGD] was the most fun I've had since I've been here."

Throughout my years of experience, in both academic and public libraries, I think that it is the small actions that I have made to help someone that really has made a huge impact. These examples are the reasons why librarians do what they do and the importance of our work. No matter how large or how small the act is, librarians are making a difference in the lives of library users every day. The needs of the community have inspired librarians to do more with less by finding creative ways to carry out the vision.

BEST PRACTICES ON IMPLEMENTING INNOVATIVE PROGRAMS AT YOUR LIBRARY

Before your library can move forward, it's imperative to understand where it has been. You will have to access your library's programs, services, resources, community, budget, facilities, staff, vision, and mission. Talk to employees and library champions about the library. What is it that your community desires from the library? What are some things that the library does well? What are some things that the library staff does well? What are some areas of improvement for the library? Look at a variety of business models and determine what will work best for your library. Understand (or develop!) the vision and mission statement for your library. Only when your vision and mission are clear, you can make steps toward carrying out the vision. Access your vision and mission regularly. Be open to change no matter how wild it may be. Try something new or different for a few months. If it does not work, that is okay. Encourage feedback from the library users and staff. Understand that not everyone will be pleased, you must take risks. Librarians and other event organizers can use this outline as a checklist to ensure successful event planning and execution.

The first step to planning an event is to start your research and planning early. It is never too soon to start the planning process.

- Planning
  - Determine the purpose of programming and outreach services for your library based on your library's mission and/or strategic plan.
  - On college campuses, identify faculty, academic departments, student groups, specialty groups, and organizations who might be interested in collaborating with the library. Tip: Get new faculty onboard. They are usually excited about their new positions and may also have less commitments than faculty who have tenure.
  - Visit the Programming Librarian website for a list of events and celebrations that gives you ideas for planning: https://programminglibrar ian.org/articles/calendar-events-celebrations.[1] This website also includes tips on copyright, funding, marketing, and more.
  - Connect with other librarians on electronic lists, social media, or visit various library websites to get ideas.
  - Hold focus groups to discover what programming the students, faculty, and staff would like to take part in.
  - Promote library resources and services.
  - Create a proposal – stay on track:
  - Outline items such as program theme, goal, venue, date, time, intended audience, length of program, budget, marketing strategy, work committee and volunteers, evaluation, and include a timeline with deliverables.

- Submit proposal to administration –timing is everything:
  - Create electronic and paper flyers.
  - Gather all participants to discuss details.

- Create a committee:
  - Meet regularly with work committee to discuss
  - Develop a communication plan with team members.
  - Develop an event timeline with due dates for each component.

- Collaborate – build partnerships in the community:
  - Identify people within the local community to assist with programming activity.
  - Use university television and radio stations, newspapers, and other local media to promote the event.
  - Reach out to marketing students and faculty at the university to see what ideas they have to assist with the marketing campaign.
  - Work with the library's communication office for event promotion.
  - Use social media tools.

o Promote programs on library website and during library instruction sessions.

- Logistics – write it down and create a work flow plan:
  o Recruit team members and place them in roles that play to their strengths.
  o Partner team members who want to learn a new role with more experienced ones.
  o Define positions and assignments clearly.
  o Review event timeline with team members.
  o Check in with team members on a weekly basis.
  o Have backup volunteers and speakers in mind in case someone cannot attend.
  o If holding an event outside, have a rain plan.
  o Invite a facilities staff member to attend a meeting; they may offer ideas and suggestions on the best way to use the space.

- Report – to illustrate best practices:
  o Record successes, challenges, and lessons learned to assist with planning for next year.
  o Share your story with others in articles, presentations, and other venues.

Some of these steps will vary depending on the size of your event and your organization's structure and culture. In this case less is not more. You want to make sure that you have as much information as possible in your proposal. If your proposal is declined, follow up with administration or your supervisor to determine why. This will help you determine if you need to improve your communication and presentation skills or perhaps there is another reason unrelated to you as to why your proposal was declined. Your proposal may get held up in administration but keep working your plan as much as you can. If you are passionate about your plan, "sell it" to your library's administration. This means help them understand why this event or activity is important, and how it will benefit the library, department, or institution as a whole. Don't be afraid to follow up with administration. Don't give up.

Do not get discouraged if a possible collaborative partner does not respond to you immediately. Give them a few days, then follow up via email, phone, or in person. Yes, you may have to actually go to their office and speak with them face-to-face or give them a call. If you are unsuccessful after three attempts, find another partner to work with.

Libraries are more than just books. They are trusted institutions that hold vital information for knowledge seekers of all backgrounds. For some people, libraries are the only reliable, welcoming, and safe resources they have consistent access to. Because of this, it is vital for all librarians to remain true to our professional mission and the communities that we serve and seek to transform.

NOTE

1. Programming Librarian. (2020, January 30). News: Calendar of events & celebrations: https://programminglibrarian.org/articles/calendar-events-celebrations.

CHAPTER 15

PUBLIC LIBRARIANS AND COMMUNITY ENGAGEMENT: THE WAY FORWARD

Meghan Moran

ABSTRACT

Public libraries are great equalizers in a society that has become more divided between those who have plenty and those who can hardly survive. Anyone is welcome in a public library – there is no need to purchase anything or show identification to be there, and you can stay if you follow the rules and the doors are open. Public librarians use their skills and knowledge to help people find information to improve and enrich their lives.

One way this happens is through community engagement. The more librarians become involved in their community, the better they can aid the community. This chapter explores how librarians can become more enmeshed within their communities, how libraries can transition from a traditional model of librarianship to a focus on meeting people where they are, both in terms of physical space and in overall skill, and how we can use technology to aid in these pursuits. The public library can be used as a bridge between the public and other services. Forward thinking ideas will help ensure the continued value that the public sees in libraries.

Keywords: Community engagement; community outreach; public libraries; communities; inclusion; library technology

Hope and a Future: Perspectives on the Impact that Librarians and Libraries Have on our World
Advances in Librarianship, Volume 48, 139–146
ISSN: 0065-2830/doi:10.1108/S0065-283020210000048015

Public libraries are one of the greatest equalizers in modern times. They are open for all to enter with no restrictions based on where someone lives, how much money they make, or any other stratification systems that generally keep people separated. This inclusivity is what makes them unique among other institutions – there is no implicit or explicit need to pay to enter, there is no restriction in terms of use, and all are welcome.

As public librarians, we have the privilege to use our skills and knowledge to help people find information they need to improve and enrich their lives. We work daily with individuals who are looking for a variety of information – from recommendations on romance novels, to finding help for someone signing up for Medicare, to information about taxes, and even about where to purchase a specific brand of shoes. Just about any question is fair game for patrons to ask, and, as librarians, we must know how to find those answers. With the wide array of people who use our services, these questions range from the mundane to the extreme, with a lot of variation in between.

One of the greatest parts of public librarianship is engaging with our users to understand what types of information they are looking for and using the questions we receive to understand our community better. Are people constantly asking about a particular book? Or a certain topic? Are we always running out of flyers that talk about domestic violence or homelessness? How can we learn from these trends and what can we do to provide quality information to our users?

Part of the answer to these questions is community engagement. The more that we as public librarians become involved in our communities, the better we can understand the community. By talking with community members and working with community partners, librarians can transition from a traditional model of librarianship to one that focuses on meeting people in the community that they serve. Public librarians can use a variety of tools at their disposal to connect and engage in meaningful ways with the community.

TYPES OF PUBLIC LIBRARY OUTREACH AND ENGAGEMENT

One of the greatest assets of public libraries is the outreach they perform within the community. Libraries perform outreach in a couple of key ways – through the delivery of materials to individuals within their community and by working with community partners to provide services and materials outside of the library. Neither of these types of outreach are new to librarianship, but their long lasting history shows the effectiveness and continued need for these services.

Home Delivery

Libraries have had book delivery services since the early 1900s. One of the most famous of these services is the Pack Horse Librarian Project, administered by the Works Progress Administration (WPA) from 1934 to 1943 (McGraw, 2017). Pack horse librarians delivered library materials to remote populations in several states, providing library services to those who otherwise would not have been easily able to access a library. Fictionalized versions of these librarians have been written about in recent years with compelling stories that detail the work of the librarians and the impact that delivering materials had on those they served. One of these novels, *The Giver of Stars*, by Jojo Moyes, focuses on two fictional characters, Margery O'Hare and Alice Van Cleve, employed as WPA Pack Horse librarians delivering library books and magazines to rural Kentuckians in the late 1930s. In the book, the two women frequently discuss their delivery routes, the people they deliver to, and news about what is going on in their town. One of the most poignant moments in the book occurs between Margery and Alice. While the two women are out shopping for supplies, Alice comments that Margery hasn't been herself for the past few days. Margery says that she had "a little upset" while on a route. In response, Alice says, "I understand. It's a tougher job than you think, sometimes, isn't it? Not really about delivering books at all" (Moyes, 2019, p. 184). What Alice says is entirely true. While the delivery of materials is extremely important, this relatively simplistic act does not encapsulate the scope of what this type of outreach involves or how it affects both the librarians and the citizens who use the service.

Community Partnerships

Another way that libraries integrate themselves fully into the community is through the formation of partnerships with other community organizations. These partnerships are a natural way for like-minded individuals who are invested in the community to join forces and create more impactful services. Not only can these partnerships be used as a way to market information about the library (and for other organizations to market their own information), but they can be a conduit for sharing community issues, exploring ways to address them, and forming plans from multiple perspectives to address diverse and complex community issues. Community organizations approach issues with varying viewpoints. Understanding what is occurring locally is of utmost importance when planning for future programs and services. It's not possible for every organization to have their thumb entirely on community needs and interests; therefore, these partnerships are essential in order to combine forces and gain a better understanding of public needs.

The Importance of These Relationships

I can only explain the importance of forming these relationships by speaking about some of my personal experiences. For the past four years, I have been delivering materials regularly to some of our library's most vulnerable populations. The individuals I deliver to are mostly senior citizens who, having worked for most of their lives, have a small amount of money coming in and often are unable to leave their homes. Many are no longer able to drive. Most live alone. Others cannot easily leave their homes due to injury or illness.

The vast majority of people I deliver to don't just want library materials though – they want a connection, a friend, someone to talk with about their lives and interests. Many had this type of interaction throughout their lives through their work, in community groups, or as library users, but no longer have the opportunity to interact with others in this way. These visits are a lifeline to the outside world, provide a connection to another member of their community, and friendship for both the recipient and librarian.

As this friendship develops, trust builds between the receiver and the deliverer. The relationship transitions from "Could you please bring me some books?" to "I haven't seen you in awhile, Meghan. We have a lot to catch up on!". In so many cases, a true friendship forms, and delivering to patrons becomes an act that, like Alice Van Cleve says, is "not really about delivering books at all" (Moyes, 2019, p. 184). The act of delivering library materials becomes a conduit to forming relationships and is an opportunity for librarians to see firsthand what members of their community are experiencing.

Because of this friendship and trust, patrons tend to feel comfortable discussing parts of their lives that they may not have otherwise talked about with librarians while visiting the library. These conversations between friends reveal deeper information needs than that which are typically discussed during a standard reference interview. Traditional reference interactions, even if they are frequent, can't build this type of relationship. Librarians have restraints on their time and are focused on finding an answer for the patron's immediate need. Patrons are in a public space with little privacy. A level of familiarity that is comfortable enough to achieve a true sense of trust is almost impossible to find in such a public setting. A traditional library setting may never allow patrons to feel comfortable enough to express their deepest information needs. By delivering to patrons, library staff break down the barriers that patrons experience and enable them to share some of their deepest needs in a way they may otherwise never have been capable of. There is a level of vulnerability involved in telling someone what your difficulties are and how you need help with them. Delivering to homes can help to overcome some of the barriers that patrons may have and allow for library workers to understand them better.

These relationships, and the knowledge that comes with them, allow librarians to better serve their communities. The job of the library staff member during these interactions is to carefully listen to challenges expressed by the patron, think of possible ways that the library could assist them, either through library work itself or through referrals to other resources that may be more appropriate for their needs, and to be watchful for trends across the community that the library may be able to address on a larger scale. It is important to make connections between the needs of the patron and the resources that the library can provide. This is extremely challenging work that requires several skills to be used at once: active listening, empathy, compassion, understanding, not to mention the resourcefulness that is required of the library staff member. The staff member must know all the ways in which the library can assist patrons through numerous complex situations. This requires a deep understanding of traditional library services and broad knowledge of community resources that can be offered in various situations.

Knowing the community resources that patrons can be referred to is an important component of working with patrons in vulnerable situations. Although resources may be available online, some patrons may not be computer literate or do not have access to a computer or the internet. Additionally, it can be difficult to determine the accuracy of online information. While many organizations do have other access points such as phone or email, they may not be continuously monitored. Phone calls or emails may not be quickly returned, especially in organizations that exist in communities with high volumes of need. When patrons need access to resources, they may not be able to do research through organization websites, make numerous phone calls, or may have trouble finding this information. The library staff member can assist patrons with this work.

One of the most effective ways I have found to know the types of services that different community organizations offer is through a community partnership group. The group I am part of meets once a month to share what is happening within their organizations, to elicit advice, and to build relationships between organizations to better serve our community. This partnership has successfully created a number of collaborative services and activities and provides a support base for organization members to rely on. Our library has successfully supported other organizations through this partnership and has been supported by our community partners.

Being part of these meetings helps our library understand what is happening within the community, what changes are being made, what services are being provided by other entities, and what opportunities exist to work with other groups. This is an effective and important relationship because keeping up with all of the groups can be a challenge. Services and resources change all the time within organizations. Communication of those changes can be slow. Emails may not be sent out reflecting changes and websites may not be updated. Depending on the size of the community, numerous organizations may have available resources which, while great in terms of volume, may elicit challenges in precisely narrowing down to the best resource for the specific situation. Having immediate knowledge about the key services that exist in the community is a helpful tool for librarians to have. Community partnerships can help make this happen.

HOW LIBRARIES CAN ENHANCE COMMUNITY ENGAGEMENT EFFORTS

Many libraries have integrated outreach into their service models but consistent improvement of these services is needed. An increased emphasis on looking to the community for guidance is necessary as is a willingness to adjust traditional library service models to allow for changes in service.

Prioritize Equity, Diversity and Inclusion Efforts

To increase efforts in community engagement, our mission must be to reach all members of the community. To do this, we must make special efforts to engage with groups that have traditionally been marginalized by libraries. Institutionalized racism exists in public libraries and librarianship as a profession. Efforts have been made at a national level through the American Library Association (ALA) to increase awareness and resources to libraries about equity, diversity, and inclusion, but these efforts need to be enacted in all communities (ALA, 2019). This will require specific strategic steps by individual public libraries. While each community will have to take different steps to ensure inclusive practices, some of these should include diverse hiring initiatives, cultural competency training for all staff, and the inclusion of the voices of traditionally marginalized community groups into the highest levels of library decision-making. In conjunction to this is the necessity for an anti-racist platform to be present in public libraries. We are not truly "public" if we are not actively seeking to include groups who have been traditionally neglected from our services.

Shifting Away from Traditional Service Models

While many public libraries have made huge efforts to engage with their communities, the traditional model of service still dominates the profession – complete with large library buildings, multiple service desks, and numerous staff in one location. As we see trends changing in how individuals look for information and use libraries, we can use some of the outreach methods to engage with users in new ways to appeal to changing needs. If public libraries continue to trend toward this route, future staffing models within public libraries may have to be revised to accommodate the changing ways our communities interact with information. There may be a time where there needs to be an equal amount of staff in the library building as well as outside of it. Creative staffing models including more overlapping roles, a minimization of service desks, or technology-aided solutions may be required to allow for more staff time, which can be dedicated to community outreach efforts.

Embrace Technology

As stated above, librarians can use technology within their libraries to free up time that can be used for community outreach. Automating processes and streamlining workflows will allow for more time to be dedicated to the complex work of community outreach. This doesn't necessarily mean hiring more staff or using expensive equipment to automate processes. It could be as simple as making small tweaks to existing workflows to facilitate library staff spending more time engaging with users and their community.

Teaching your staff about available technology options in your library can also be useful. Instructing your staff in technology troubleshooting and about the technology tools that are easily accessible to them will empower them to use these tools regularly and give them other options with which to create unique programs and services. Participating in community engagement is thoughtful work and cannot be rushed. Using technology can help assist in this endeavor and allow for more time to spend with your patrons.

Successful Examples

Every library differs in the programs and services required to reach their communities. I can only speak to successful experiences I have had that helped me to enhance my library's community outreach and engagement efforts. Through streamlining workflows, teaching staff more about technology, and providing staff training on multiple processes, I have repurposed time in our schedule to assist in community engagement efforts. Some of these efforts include:

- Forming partnerships with nonprofit organizations. By doing so we were able to offer resume-building programs conducted by library staff to benefit their clients in job hunting, provide collaborative programs target to senior citizens, and embed librarians at regular community meetings for several organizations to answer questions and raise awareness about library services.
- Participating in our local hospital's community health council. By evaluating data presented by their health team, We became aware of the need to address and offer information to our community on the opioid crisis. We created a series of library programs to inform the public about this critical issue that is affecting many in our community. Several community experts participated in these programs and provided valuable information and resources to our patrons. One of the programs featured poignant stories of community members directly affected by this issue.
- Creating a user experience team to engage with patrons in order to learn more about how they use the library. This helps us enhance our services to effectively understand user needs and find creative solutions in library services to meet them.

While these efforts have been successful, there is still more work to be done. In fact, this is the type of work that never ends. There will always be opportunities to learn more about what our patrons need. It's our obligation to listen to their concerns and enact changes that will benefit all.

THE POWER OF LIBRARIES

Public libraries exist because communities have pooled their resources to fund them, build them, and use them. These spaces have been created as an open place for all where knowledge can be shared with one another, where trained professionals can help find needed information, and where new skills can be learned to improve lives.

As public librarians, we have the honor of serving the public. Our greatest hope is that we can help anyone in our community find what they need to make their life a little bit better. We are open to all. We provide accurate information to anyone who needs it. We work collaboratively with our community to provide the best set of resources available to meet the community's needs. Jenny Bossaller (2018) states that "being a member of a community includes a sense of belonging. Public libraries are a place for people to belong – culturally and intellectually, regardless of their backgrounds" (p. 310). Public libraries help to build this sense of community belonging, and community engagement is essential in doing so.

REFERENCES

American Library Association (ALA). (2019). Equity, diversity, and inclusion. Retrieved from http://
    www.ala.org/advocacy/diversity

Bossaller, J. S. (2018). Collaboration and consortia. In K. de la Peña McCook & J. S. Bossaller (Eds.),
    Introduction to public librarianship (3rd ed., pp. 293–320). Chicago, IL: ALA Neal-Schuman.

McGraw, E. (2017). Horse-riding librarians were the great depression's bookmobiles. Retrieved from
    https://www.smithsonianmag.com/history/horse-riding-librarians-were-great-depression-
    bookmobiles-180963786/

Moyes, J. (2019). *The giver of stars*. New York, NY: Viking.

INDEX